Overcoming
Personal Loss

Overcoming Personal Loss

Duane E. Hiatt

Deseret Book Company
Salt Lake City, Utah

Library of Congress Cataloging-in-Publication Data

Hiatt, Duane E.
Overcoming personal loss / by Duane E. Hiatt.
    p. cm.
   ISBN 0-87579-309-6
   1. Consolation. 2. Spiritual life—Mormon authors. 3. Hiatt,
Duane E. I. Title.
BX8656.H52 1990
248.8'6—dc20   90-30820
                                      CIP

Printed in the United States of America

10   9   8   7   6   5   4   3   2

To Diane and Sharon
and
Daniel, Robert, Joseph, David,
John, Matthew, Angela, Callie,
Samuel, Benjamin, Kathryn,
Thomas, Joshua, Lucy, and Maren,
who are helping me turn my
losses into eternal victories

Contents

Contents

Part 3: Overcoming, Not Just Enduring

Part 4: The Value of Loss in Our Lives

Preface

No one lives without loss; it is part of life. But loss can affect us in different ways. To some it is nourishment, to others poison. Some it cripples, others it strengthens. The difference lies not in the loss but in the way we respond to it. If we settle into despair, the darkness will gather ever deeper around us. But if we stagger forward and grope toward the light, we will find our steps gradually stronger and more sure. The journey is always uphill and usually hard. But when we arrive back in the light, we are better people for having made the trek.

The road up from loss, like other roads, is easier traveled with a map and markers along the way. The journey is lighter with friends to share the burden and encourage us with stories of their own struggles and successes. The purpose of this book is to help provide that guidance, encouragement, and inspiration for you or for someone you care about who has suffered a loss.

Acknowledgments

Carol Christensen, my assistant at Brigham Young University, took hours of her own time to counsel with me and evaluate the material in this book. Carol also typed, retyped, corrected, and recorrected the manuscript. I am deeply grateful for her skill, wisdom, and willingness.

Sheri Dew, my editor at Deseret Book, invited me to write this book and guided it through to completion. Her insights, experience, and encouragement have been most helpful. I would also like to thank Emily Watts, my copy editor at Deseret Book.

Many people willingly shared their stories and their strength with me as I worked through my own greatest loss and gathered material to help others work through theirs. I am grateful to them.

Introduction

· ·

Overcoming your loss will be a journey. To make that journey successfully you will need three things. First, you will need a map to show you the direction and to point out goals to guide your course. Second, you will need to know the steps that will move you along to your destination. Third, you will need fuel to give you power for your journey.

This journey in overcoming your loss is part of the larger pilgrimage that is life itself. It is largely a trip you must make alone. But sometimes a traveling companion can help pass the lonely hours and give you encouragement. I hope I can be that companion for you in this book.

I would not presume to know your feelings, and it is not my intent to impose my opinions and judgments on your situation. Your loss is unique because you are unique. But you will go through certain stages along the journey in overcoming your loss, stages that are typical of every person who overcomes a loss. These stages can help you recognize where you are in the overcoming process and give you encouragement as you see the progress you are making. I have described in this book three such stages in the process of overcoming your loss.

The first stage comes with the first numbing pains of your loss. The second stage is the long, gray grind as you reconstruct your life to include the loss which is now a part of you. The third stage is overcoming. In this stage you deal with loss not as a permanent setback, but as a part of the process of your eternal growth toward godhood.

As you pass through these stages, you will make better progress if you have goals to reach. Experienced outdoor survivors know that a person can travel through wilderness best by taking a general compass heading, then picking out a visible goal and working toward it. By traveling from goal to goal you finally reach your destination. This book is structured around this goal-reaching concept.

I have identified some short-term survival goals at the beginning of each stage of our progress. These goals, called "Milestone Markers," are worded in personal terms, statements you might make about yourself. I listed them at the beginning because I feel they will act as road maps for you as you make your progress through that stage in the process of overcoming your loss. These goals may look intimidating and overwhelming at first. You may say to yourself, "I am not that way. I don't have that strength or that outlook." That response is perfectly natural, and probably true. If you were in Los Angeles looking at a road map to New York City, you could say, "I am not in New York City. I'm not even in Denver or Chicago or somewhere else along the way." This would be true, but given enough time and sufficient steps or revolutions of wheels in the right direction, you would eventually get to your destination. So, as you look at the "Milestone Markers" sections at the beginning of each stage of your progress, look at them as goals to arrive at later, not as attributes you already possess.

Sitting and staring at a map will not bring us to our destination. We must take the steps to get ourselves there. So at the end of each section I have listed specific things to do, titled "Traveling Tips." These are mind, heart, and body movements that can transport us one step at a time along the journey of overcoming our loss. If we repeat them, they will become part of us.

There is one more element that is vital for our journey. That is the fuel to move us along our way. Cars, planes, trains, and ships move on the power of gasoline, oil, diesel, coal, and sometimes nuclear energy. People are propelled on the fuel of ideas, which can generate motivating emotions. These emotions ignite a spiritual fire within us to keep us moving.

Loss drains our energy and our emotions. It often takes from us those things which seem to make life worth living. It turns life's bright colors into gray, life's music into monotones, and it makes us wonder what is the use of even trying. To overcome loss we need to refuel our tanks, recharge our batteries, and reignite our fires. We need new ideas, new inspirations, new perspectives and ways of looking at life. The motivational fuel in this book is between the goal sections, "Milestone Markers," and the activities sections, "Traveling Tips." Between these two I have described the best ideas I know to overcome loss. I have found and continue to find them very helpful.

One last comment: I know that giving counsel to others is a risky business. There is always the danger of sounding condescending or overly simple. I hope nothing in this book sounds like a pat on the head or a minimizing of your loss. If it does, I apologize. Like you, I am constantly struggling with life's losses, large and small, and trying to turn them into the ultimate success the Lord intended our lives to be.

Overcoming Loss –
a Personal Story

I looked down again at the little yellow card in my hand. It was dog-eared from being taken out of my planning book every day. On the bottom of the card I read my handwritten note, "Turn every lemon into lemonade." I laughed a long, hollow, empty laugh that turned to sobs at the end. How ridiculous it seemed to battle the dragon of death with the puny sword of human optimism.

Time to ponder, even time to weep, is a luxury when you have a terminally ill wife and fifteen children. The tear reservoirs are soon emptied, and the dry sobs soon lose their ability to tap off the pressure on your mind and heart. Then it is time to get up and put one foot in front of the other. I picked up my briefcase and left the office.

I climbed into my faithful but aging pickup truck. I eased it out of park, which didn't really hold anymore, into drive and gently pushed the accelerator. The truck had once been a husky, three-quarter-ton with a heavy, cast-iron block and four hundred cubic inches of plunging horsepower. Its mechanical muscles were starting to sag from the many miles it had traveled. It, too, was losing life. Everything about me seemed a harbinger of death.

Diane met me at the door. She smiled with tired eyes and thin lips. We embraced, and both of us tried not to notice the growing bulge at her middle coming between us. Sometimes, we could almost imagine it was another pregnancy, like the ones we had worked through together. But those swellings had been filled with life. This one, we knew, was filled with death.

We savored every moment we could be together during the following weeks. The cancer swelled within her. I contacted every resource we thought might help. Every therapy and technique I was told about or read about I traced down and called. I found that in the traditional medical circles as well as the nontraditional, and even the folk remedies and unproved therapies, there is much more heat than light. Everybody knows something about cancer, but nobody knows enough. Each side blames the other for malpractice in treating the disease, but no one really knows what to do.

She had ovarian cancer. This is rare in a woman still bearing children, as she was. When they operated and removed the tumor, they felt they had gotten it all. We agreed to radiation treatments of the affected area to make sure the cancer was killed. The treatments were hard on her constitution and digestive system, but they seemed to do the job. For several months she seemed cancer free. But then a routine checkup X-ray showed a tiny, dark spot on her liver. A particle of the tumor, probably just a few cells, had broken free before the operation and floated into her liver. It was inoperable. She had received all the radiation her body could handle, and we chose not to put her through the harsh effects of chemotherapy. There were no other options in traditional medical therapy.

We tried diet, homeopathic, and other remedies. They may have helped some and slowed the cancer down, but nothing killed it. Diane grew weaker, thinner in all but her bloated liver. The blessings I gave her every morning kept down the pain but did not stop the growth of the malignancy. We chose to care for her at home with the help of home health services and a gentle, devoted nurse named Carol Lastowski.

Our third son, Joe, came home from his studies and work in Philadelphia. Robert, our second son, came from Arizona. Our fourth son, David, was counseled to stay on his mission in California, which he did. Our oldest son, Dan, and his wife were unable to come in from Japan. We gathered about Diane, talked with her, and listened to her last intelligible words. Then she grew too weak to utter more than simple requests for water.

One morning three weeks later, as I slept on the floor beside her bed, I had an unusual dream of travel and flight around and away from earth. I awoke and did not have to stir from my pillow to know that she was gone. I knew it even before I realized that her labored breathing had stopped. Examining her, I found no pulse. The disfiguring swelling of her abdomen had already begun to recede. The cancer in its perverse nature had consumed its victim, and now would die itself. I called my neighbor Dr. Keith Hooker; he came and pronounced her dead. Then I called a mortician.

As I waited for him, I called the children. We met around the body of their mother. I told them to feel free to cry, now or whenever they needed to in the future, that I had cried and would cry again. But no one cried then. I said, "Your mother is not far away, even now. She is looking upon this scene and upon us and comforting us. We will see her and know her and be with her again. But for a time she has another work that she needs to do. We must carry on here. We will be together again in the future."

The older children held the little ones in their arms. We talked about whatever they wanted to talk about. Mostly we discussed what it means to be alive, what happens when we pass from this life to the next life through the portal that closes here and opens there — the door we call death. I told them, "Death has been pictured in an ugly mask by the superstitious and through horror stories and movies. But really, as you can see, it is a gentle, quiet thing. Your mother's face was twisted in pain, but now it is relaxed. Her spirit, which was trapped in a diseased and helpless body, is now free — more free than ours."

And so we talked and waited until the mortician came and took her away. Then we talked again. I have talked with the children many times since then, together and individually. Four-year-old Lucy, who watched in dry-eyed interest the work of the morticians, later came to me in a quiet moment. "Daddy," she said, "I cried when they took Mama away. I cried inside."

"So did I, Lucy. So did I," I said.

At the end of that day, as we gathered for scripture reading and prayer, I complimented the children on having survived the hardest day of our lives. Looking back, I think that is still true. There would be the day of the funeral and burial. There would be the long, gray days of that hot summer. There would be our first Christmas without our mother. These were all hard, but I still believe the first day was the hardest.

It has been a tradition for as long as our children can remember that each night after scriptures and prayers they answer two questions. The first is, "What was your happiest thing today?" The second, for the children over eight years of age, is, "What did you do to build the Lord's kingdom today?" It might have seemed out of place, but I asked those questions again that night. The children all gave identical answers. "My happiest thing is that I know I will be with Mom again. What I did for the kingdom was I made it through the day."

"That's good," I said. "That is enough."

The experts in these matters say that I as a husband and we as a family had suffered one of the worst psychological and emotional traumas in the book. I don't know how such a loss compares with the loss of a child, a close parent or sibling, a divorce, or with physical impairments — blindness, deafness, paralysis. I don't know how you would go about comparing them. So much depends on the individual circumstance. But I know that this is a big one. I set aside a year in which to get my head back together. I read later that the average is two years in America: that's how long it takes before the accident and suicide rates of surviving spouses return to normal. I'm not suicide prone, but I wouldn't have trusted myself with any complicated or dangerous equipment for a while. I stumbled around a lot, and my mind was mostly elsewhere for a long time. I understood for the first time how one could prefer to be in the next life rather than this one. If it had not been for the children and for whatever work I am supposed to accomplish in this life, I would have preferred to move on.

Many dark dawns I stood at Diane's grave and thought deeply. Sometimes I sank to my knees and wept hot tears on the cold headstone. But then I would have to stand up and plod homeward to the children and my work. Often I quoted aloud the words of Robert Frost from "Stopping by Woods on a Snowy Evening." I had memorized them years before but never understood them until now:

> *The woods are lovely, dark and deep.*
> *But I have promises to keep,*
> *And miles to go before I sleep,*
> *And miles to go before I sleep.*

The cemetery is on my morning jogging route, so I stop at Diane's grave most mornings. I often used to think, with a grim smile, "With the rotten, healthy lifestyle I keep, I could go on down here for another half century." The thought did not particularly appeal to me.

Gradually, over the weeks and months, my desire to die dissipated. I picked up the threads of my life and began to reweave them into a new tapestry. A beautiful new strand in the pattern appeared when Sharon Lee Johnson consented to be my wife. I know that the blessing of remarriage does not come to every person who loses a spouse to death or divorce. If you don't get the chance to remarry, probably your recovery from loss will be harder than mine was, but I believe it is still possible. Recovery does not mean reconstruction of what you had or what you were before. That is impossible. But it does mean making the most of the new condition in which you find yourself.

This is the situation in our family now. None of us are the same people we were. We still think of Diane often and pray for her every night and morning, but we don't weep when we do. We have survived and even gained a little ground in our quest for salvation and exaltation, I believe.

Whether your loss is a loved one, a marriage, a physical ability, an opportunity, a job, a hope or dream — the process of overcoming it will be somewhat similar. In the pages that follow, I have described that process from my experience and the experiences of others, and shared some thoughts in the hope that they may help you as they have helped me.

Part 1

The First
Numbing Pains

Milestone Markers

The most important goals we will achieve in this life are the character traits that will move us along toward our ultimate destination, which is to be like our Heavenly Father and to dwell with him. Loss can move us closer to, or farther from, this destination.

Following are some emotional, mental, and physical attributes toward which you are heading as you begin your journey working through the first numbing pains of loss. Down the road of your journey, you will at some point be able to say these statements and believe them:

I can outlast this painful period, and I know that sooner or later it will pass.

Every moment, every hour, every day that I endure this pain is a victory for me, for time is on my side.

I have suffered a loss, but I am not bitter about it.

I am a strong person; I can stand up under this loss.

I have internal psychological and emotional resources that will get me through this hard time.

I am loved by my family, my friends, and most importantly and certainly by my Heavenly Father and by my Savior, Jesus Christ.

I am beginning to adjust to my new situation and find it at least bearable.

I am beginning to form productive habits in my life to accommodate the loss without having it destroy my life. These habits may include new activities, new schedules, new contacts and associates.

I am beginning to picture and focus in my mind a lifestyle that will include my loss but will not be dominated and directed by it.

I am taking confidence and courage as I look back at the hard things in my life I have endured thus far.

I am beginning to map out on paper, or at least in my mind, positive directions my life will take now that I have endured the first part of my loss.

I have developed greater trust and deeper love for my Father in heaven as I have seen how he has helped me get through this difficult time in my life.

Through prayer and contemplation, I have developed a deeper appreciation for my own inner strengths and reserves. This has helped me become a more calm and confident person.

Nothing I will face now or in the future will crush me, because my Savior will sustain me.

Chapter 1

It's Okay to Cry

. . . .

My friend took my hand in both of his. His gaunt face was etched with the deep lines of eighty-plus years of living. His blue eyes were clouded and watery, as the eyes of old people become. His face was deeply lined from the strain he had borne up under the last few years caring for his wife as she slowly died of leukemia. Now she was breathing her last, and I had come as her bishop to give her a final blessing.

Her devoted husband followed me outside her hospital room to take my hand and thank me for coming. "It was so kind of you to come and . . . " His voice cracked as the sobs welled up in his throat. He dropped his eyes, a little embarrassed. "I'm sorry. I didn't mean to lose control, but she is a wonderful wife. And sixty-three years together is a long time."

I nodded, gave his weathered hands a final squeeze, and walked down the hospital corridor. I didn't say to him what I was thinking. It didn't seem appropriate at the moment. I wanted to say, "Don't apologize. I am just sorry you don't feel free to pour out your feelings in any way that may help. If a man can't weep over the loss of his beloved, lifetime companion, why were we born with tear ducts anyway?"

The Doctrine and Covenants counsels us to "weep for the loss of them that die." (D&C 42:45.) This is good spiritual and psychological practice. Crying can help to tap off the emotional pressure that builds up in a time of loss.

Our society puts rather strict limits on what is considered a proper display of feelings. A few years ago Edmund Muskie, the U.S. Senator from Maine, was a viable presidential candidate. At one fateful news conference, in a moment of failure and frustration, he let fall a tear or two. He was politically dead from that moment. In the minds of the press and public, he was the crying candidate. The same thing happened a few years later to a female member of the U.S. House of Representatives. She was, if anything, even more sharply criticized than Muskie, because it was said she had betrayed not only herself but her sex, giving the impression that women were not tough enough to handle the highest political offices.

Most of us grow up in fear of taunts and teasing if we let our emotions show. "Crybaby," "wimp," "sob sister," and other epithets are hurled at us when we are small, and they leave a lasting impression about how we should behave. So we squeeze off the tear ducts, bottle the emotion, and try to take it on the chin without showing outwardly how much it hurts.

Given our society, that's probably a practical approach — in public. But in private and within ourselves, it is well to remember that crying is often a sign of sensitivity and compassion, not weakness. The shortest verse in the Bible reminds us that the Lord himself is not above showing emotion. John 11:35 records simply, "Jesus wept."

The Lord's prophets also show their pain with tears. In a stake conference in the Provo Utah Edgemont Stake in the spring of 1987, Elder Paul H. Dunn told of being in Hawaii on a church assignment with President Harold B. Lee. Late one night he heard a soft knock on his door. When he opened it, President Lee collapsed into his arms sobbing, "Help me, please help me." President Lee had just learned of the death of his daughter. Elder Dunn learned a great lesson at that moment. If a great and strong man like Harold B. Lee, the Lord's prophet, can weep over his loss, the invitation is open to us all.

President Lee later wrote that his tears gushed forth anew when he descended from the airplane in Salt Lake City and saw the little motherless family before him. He gathered his grand-children about him and cried again, but they did not cry. He said to them, "Here your grandpa is crying and you are not."

They replied, "Grandpa, we have cried and cried until we are all out of tears."

Eventually the tears do dry, but, like little mountain springs, they may refresh themselves after a while and run again for a time. All the familiar things of your world that once were your friends may seem like adversaries for a time. If your loss was financial, it's pretty obvious that you won't find the same zest in looking at your books when the bottom lines are red as you did when they were black. If your loss is a physical ability, the tennis shoes or dancing shoes you once enjoyed slipping on may be a source of pain when you see them from a wheelchair or a bed. If you have lost love and companionship through a divorce, those treasured wedding pictures and mementoes that once made you misty-eyed may do so again, but not in the same way. If a loved one has died, every drawer and closet will probably hold a painful surprise, causing a catch in your throat and more tears.

There are more and less effective ways to use crying in over-coming grief. The same thing could be said for any mental or emotional technique. Used alone and to excess, most tools become ineffective, even counterproductive. It's hard to hammer with a saw or saw with a hammer. Too much "stiff upper lip" can wear us down and wear us out in the face of adversity. Sometimes we need to bend a little or we will break. Too much leaning on our support systems can deprive us of the opportunity to build our own strength, but the support of others is practically indispensable as we are working our way back from a loss.

Likewise, too much crying can produce a psychological syn-drome similar to the self-fulfilling prophecy. We cry because we are hurt or grief stricken. If we continue to cry, and only cry, as a response to our sadness, the crying itself can become a source of sadness. We say to ourselves, "I must have suffered great — perhaps irreparable — damage, because see how much I am crying." The cycle of crying because we are sad and being sad because we are crying can repeat itself unendingly unless we interrupt it with some of the other techniques of healing and recovery, which will be discussed later in this book.

Crying alone will not bring about the healing we need when we hurt from a loss, but used in conjunction with other mental and emotional rehabilitation, it can be very helpful. It can release the bottled-up pressure and pain that come with the first shocks of our loss. It can remind us that we are human and vulnerable, sometimes even helpless, before the powers of other elements in our existence. This realization can open the door to humility and trust in God, who has all power, all wisdom, perfect love for us as his children, and a Father's desire to give us only what is ultimately for our best good.

Used for these purposes, crying can help us endure and overcome our loss. We will find after a time that we do not need to cry anymore; our tears have served their purpose. Eventually, we will find that the grief itself will pass. We will discover the wisdom and truth in the words of Psalm 30:5, "Weeping may endure for a night, but joy cometh in the morning."

Chapter 2

What Happened?

. . . .

What happened?

"It was the best thing that could have happened to our family. The experience pulled us together, helped to unite us in a bond of common purpose, and showed us what the truly important things in life are—our loved ones and our families. It helped to bring our children back, and it helped me to focus my life on what is really most important to me."

"For what is a man profited, if he shall gain the whole world, and lose his own soul?" (Matthew 16:26.)

What happened?

"I learned to love in ways I had never known before. My heart has expanded in love, not only to those who are easy to love and who love me in return, but to those who do not reciprocate my love. I have learned to love even my enemies."

"But I say unto you, Love your enemies, bless them that curse you, do good to them that hate you . . . and persecute you." (Matthew 5:44.)

What happened?

"That experience helped us take our eyes off the things of this world and concentrate on the things of eternity. It created a bond between us and heaven which is like a rope pulling us upward."

"Let the solemnities of eternity rest upon your minds." (D&C 43:34.)

What happened?

"It gave me an appreciation of life that I never had before. I wake up in the morning, take a deep breath, give thanks to God for this beautiful day, and resolve to make the best of every minute of it."

"This is the day which the Lord hath made; we will rejoice and be glad in it." (Psalm 118:24.)

What happened to each of these people? Apparently, it was something important and good. Their lives were changed for the better, and they are in the process of reaping eternal benefits from their experiences. Yet none of them would have chosen to go through these experiences.

"It pulled our family together and showed us what was really important in life," Martin said. Martin lived just up the hill from us. "Up the hill" often has meaning beyond the geographical in our location; it often means up the economic ladder as well. Martin had climbed both the hill and the economic ladder quite successfully. He was a professional man in southern California with a thriving practice and a comfortable financial portfolio, but he was also a conscientious father. He cared about his family and was concerned about the environment they were growing up in, so he moved them back to Utah to be among the Saints. He knew, as we do, that there is sin in the valleys of the mountains, just as there is everywhere else in the world. But he felt that living where there was a higher concentration of Mormons would be helpful.

To maintain the lifestyle to which he and his family had been accustomed, he still needed that income from his California clientele, so he commuted back and forth to work—flying to California for the week and returning home on weekends. This was a difficult arrangement, and he longed to be financially independent so he could stay at home with his family in Utah. Finally, the opportunity came for him to put his life savings into an extremely high-yield investment. Things were working out so well for him, it seemed too good to be true. It was. He lost everything. He was forced to return with his family to California and essentially start over. They had to sell their beautiful homes, their fine cars, and their expensive country club memberships.

After a while, they did save enough to go to Disneyland. Walking between the pirate ride and the Matterhorn with his happy children gathered close around him, Martin said, "I would never have chosen to go through that, but it's the best thing that ever happened to our family. It's not where you live; it's how you live and how much you love each other that matter. This experience has brought us together."

Mirna was a loving wife and mother of five children. Her husband left her and the children and married his secretary. She was understandably bewildered and bitter. They had been a model Latter-day Saint family. Now she felt they were more like something out of a TV soap opera or a bad novel. She alternately criticized herself for having done something wrong to ruin their marriage, although she didn't know what, and condemned the "rat of a husband" who would do such a rotten thing to his wife and children. Finally, she said, "This is getting me nowhere. I've got to change."

It wasn't easy. She fasted and prayed for the Lord to soften her heart and give her understanding. She still doesn't know why their marriage broke up, but she has learned something even more valuable. She has learned to turn this tragedy from a festering spiritual wound cankering her soul into a Gethsemane experience on the road to salvation. "Over the years the Lord has helped me learn to love my husband's new wife as a daughter of God and a sister of mine, and to regain love for my former husband—not as my husband, but as the father of our children—and to respect him in that position."

Thelma was so busy as the mother of a large family and the ward Relief Society president that she forgot to check behind the car that dreadful day when she backed out of the driveway. The terrible thump under the wheels and the sight of her own child dying in the driveway still haunts her thoughts and dreams occasionally. But the guilt and the stabbing pains to a mother's heart are finally gone. She no longer makes those accusations against herself and against the angels who should have been sent to protect her little one. His gentle voice is silent no more. It is speaking to her from the other side of the veil, constantly encouraging her and her family to live righteously so they can be together again.

"Paul's death is not bitter to me anymore. Instead, it is a gentle tug to all of us. The things of this world are not nearly so important to me – only the things of eternity and being together forever with our family."

Howard was getting along in years, but he still led and loved the active life. When that crushing pain settled on his chest one night, he knew it was all over. A triple bypass and weeks of recuperation saved his life, but left him, in his own estimation, an invalid. For a long time he wondered why God didn't just let him die and get it over with instead of confining him to the living death of a wheelchair, walker, and finally careful and measured steps to protect his weakened heart. He has found out since that there is still much work for him to do, and many joys to be experienced. Things don't have to be done at a sprinter's pace.

"That heart attack mellowed me out. It showed me blessings in this life that I'd been going by too fast to notice – things like the love of my family and friends, and like taking a breath and seeing the sun come up in the morning. Life means more to me than it did before my heart attack."

All of these people, and tens of thousands like them every day, face terrible losses in their lives. None of us will escape such experiences as these. Yet these people turned their tragedies into triumphs. Their accomplishments were difficult; they took time and tremendous effort. The process was not easy, nor was it automatic. But it worked for them, and it can work for us when we face similar trials.

When we truly overcome our losses, we don't just endure. We don't just hobble along as wounded warriors in life's battles. We are not talking here about positive mental attitude in the face of difficulties, or of painting the clouds with sunshine. These are important skills and steps along the way, but we are talking about actually transforming the clouds from thundering, menacing, drenching overcasts to floating, white banners in a blue sky – guiding us back to God, even as they led the ancient children of Israel.

It is possible to make such transformations and such redefinitions in our troubled minds and our scarred souls following a loss.

The first thing we have to do, I believe, is to define what happened to us. This may seem like a basic and overly simple question, but it is the beginning of the process in coming back from a loss. If we don't know exactly what it is we have lost, how can we recover from our loss or compensate for it? It is surprising that this basic question is usually not asked. When we suffer a setback, perhaps we want to turn our attention away from the loss as quickly as possible. It is a source of pain and grief to us, and we may not want to analyze and probe our loss.

But I suspect there is a more basic reason we rarely ask what happened. The fact is, we rarely probe for the realities of anything in our lives. We live in a world of carefully crafted facades and images. We often have reality presented to us shrouded in slogans, symbols, and stereotypes. We elect our public officials on catchy phrases and party platforms. We buy our food based more on packaging and taste than nutritional content. We purchase homes and pay for them most of our lives without knowing much about construction. Advertisers make handsome profits when they can re-create our reality to include a need for their products. We often choose our lifestyles, our political parties, even our religions, on the basis of propaganda and information that is several steps removed from reality.

Being seduced out of hard-earned money by accepting other people's versions of reality can be unfortunate, but it isn't the most serious misinterpretation we make. For example, we might kill ourselves with lung cancer while trying to impersonate the image of a virile man with a tattoo on his arm and a cigarette in his fingers. The reality is that nicotine cuts down circulation and limits all the masculine and virile functions.

This propensity for accepting illusion as reality is part of our human equipment, and generally we get along all right in the world because everybody else is thinking in about the same terms. But occasionally, during deep crisis in our lives, we will be well ahead if we pull ourselves up short, force ourselves to look into the situation, and find out what really happened.

I can hear you getting irritated with me already. I don't blame you. You're saying, "This is stupid. I know what happened. My father died," or "I was crippled in an accident," or "Business reversals wiped out an entire lifetime of hard work." Whatever the loss, it is easy to assume we know what happened. That is the first pitfall to watch out for. We have to define what *really* happened to us if we are to begin to know how to deal with it. As we do this defining, we would be well advised to examine the basis of our definitions. We would be wise to separate the observable facts from the interpretations we attach to them. We will make these interpretations despite ourselves — that is the nature of human beings. But we need to examine closely the basis on which we make those interpretations. We can define our loss as anything from emotional annihilation to a stimulating challenge spurring us on to greater accomplishment.

One night the New Jersey sky turned orange as flames exploded and burned the laboratories of Thomas A. Edison. Up in smoke went half a lifetime of ideas and experiments. It was a tragic loss. Or was it? It's a little presumptuous of us to make that statement without asking Edison. So let's look at what he saw. Standing silhouetted against the roaring flames, he sent someone for his wife, saying, "Tell her to come quickly or she'll miss one of the most spectacular fires she will ever see." Later he said, "This will give us a chance to make a whole new start." Was Edison's interpretation of these events the "real" one, or was he merely making something up to help himself and others feel better? Who has the authority to say which is the "real" interpretation of that event? Surely Edison himself should be granted that prerogative, since it is his life. And thus it is with us. Ultimately it is not the sympathizers, the mourners, or the encouragers, well-meaning though they may be, who can tell us what really happened. We must decide for ourselves. And the reality of the situation will, in large measure, rest on our ideas.

The Savior said to the Prophet Joseph Smith, "And truth is knowledge of things as they are, and as they were, and as they are to come." (D&C 93:24.) This is applicable to our interpretation of the loss we have experienced. What did we have? What is our current status, and, most important, what will the future hold? It is hard to imagine a different, better future when we have sustained a loss. The future portends to be a dark and dismal corridor down which we will drag one flagging footstep after another. But this is a false perception of reality. The future may be better or it may be worse, but it will not be the same as the present. The decision is largely in our hands — or, more precisely, in our minds — whether the future will be better than our present saddened situation.

Using your mind as an interpreter of reality and taking into consideration time and change, what do you perceive is the actual nature of your loss? If it is a business loss, it may at first appear to be a waste of years of your life, of carefully accumulated capital — perhaps a heavy burden of debt as you try to cover your losses. This is one interpretation. Can you reinterpret reality in your mind to see your loss as also a change in direction? Might you now, as a result, learn and continue in this work or some other with more insight and understanding? Such feelings and plans are difficult to develop during the pain of loss, but they do open up a shaft of light at the end of the present tunnel. Since the sun is going to come up every day regardless, we might as well greet it, looking forward to future gains rather than looking back and grieving over our losses.

That is reality if our mind chooses to make it so.

Chapter 3

What's Left after Loss?

· ·

Cy Perkins had lost a lot. Maybe no more than many other people approaching age eighty, but that is a lot. He had lost his wife, his youth, much of his mobility, his chances for fame and prosperity — and he had just lost a spirited argument. Well, sort of lost. His parting shot was, "Well, you may be right now. But when I get home, I'll be right!" With only his cat to dispute him there, Cy knew his opinion would prevail.

Despite Cy's apparent losses, he wasn't down. He was his usual twinkle-eyed, philosophical self as he continued picking the peaches on the East Sharon Stake Welfare Farm. Our ladders were close together, and I suspected there might be more than peaches to be harvested here. There might be wisdom as well. So I said, "Cy, how do you do it? How do you keep from getting down when you lose something precious to you?"

"Don't think about what I've lost," he said. "I think about what I've got left."

When Lehi's family was trudging through the Arabian desert, their steel bows lost their spring. The pessimistic older brothers, Laman and Lemuel, focused on that loss and turned it into a loss of hope in survival. They were ready to sit down and starve to death on the spot. Nephi focused on what they had left, including their ingenuity, their brains and strength, and their faith in God. Soon he had fashioned a new bow of wood and went back to hunting for food. Likewise, the focus of our attention in a time

of loss can be for us the difference between emotionally suc-
cumbing or surviving.

It isn't easy to focus on the positive. The sore-thumb
syndrome is a real factor when we face a loss. You smack your
finger with a hammer, and all of a sudden your whole attention
is focused on that blackened fingernail. The whole universe seems
to point to your pain. The same is true when we suffer a loss.
We usually center an inordinate amount of attention on the loss,
ignoring what we have left. Here is one of the most practical
exercises I know for breaking this syndrome. It is simple but very
effective.

Take a paper and pencil and write down all the good things
you have in life. Write down your health, such as it may be;
your friends; your mental faculties; knowledge, information, and
wisdom you have gained through experience and study. Usually,
the more detailed your list, the more helpful it is to you. So, for
example, instead of just listing friends as an asset, list them individually by name. You may even want to list some of their
characteristics, their smile, or a mannerism that brightens your
life. Instead of just listing health, think about your ears that catch
the music of the world, your eyes that see. Even if they don't see
as well as they once did, be grateful for what they do see. You
may want to list specific memories that you call back to add to
the richness of your life's present period. Make the list as long as
time and recollection will allow. You will find that writing one
good thing triggers thoughts of a whole bouquet of blessings blos-
soming out from that one.

Just making the list and contemplating it can ease the pain
of your loss and put it into perspective. Certainly you would want
to list as one of your greatest retained possessions a knowledge
of the gospel, because this knowledge can show us that no loss
is permanent. Every good thing will be restored to us in the proper
time.

But you can make this experience even more powerful and
helpful to you. Take that pencil and scribble out each one of those
blessings. As you do so, in your mind's eye, see this being taken

from your life, leaving an empty void. Now look at your life and consider your state. Picture yourself with none of the assets and blessings on your list. Imagine what your life would be like if this were truly the case. Live in that bleak world for a few moments. While you are here in this unhappy state you have created, use a little empathy as well. Realize that everything you have scratched out on your paper is being suffered by some people in this world. There are those who are without friends, others without freedom, many without health, some whose minds have been destroyed by disease or accident. There is no deprivation you have imagined that is not being suffered in actuality by some people in this world.

While you are in a sympathetic and sensitive state, picture Joseph Smith in a jail ironically named Liberty. In Liberty Jail the Prophet Joseph cried out in agony and desperation to the Lord, "O God, where art thou? And where is the pavilion that covereth thy hiding place? How long shall thy hand be stayed, and thine eye, yea thy pure eye, behold from the eternal heavens the wrongs of thy people and of thy servants, and thine ear be penetrated with their cries?" (D&C 121:1–2.) Joseph had legitimate cause to cry out for relief. Instead of seeing the kingdom roll forth to fill the earth as he had anticipated, based on the revelations the Lord had given him, Joseph saw it being crushed by oppression from without and apostasy from within. Joseph and the Saints had apparently lost their inheritance in the land of Zion. They had lost their homes and their possessions, and some had lost their lives. Joseph had lost friends, his family had been ripped from him, and he was on the verge of losing hope.

The Lord answered his anguished pleas with gentleness and wisdom. He counseled Joseph to do the same thing we are suggesting here—to try to avoid thinking of his loss and concentrate on what he had left and how he might build upon it. The Lord said, "My son, peace be unto thy soul; thine adversity and thine afflictions shall be but a small moment; and then, if thou endure it well, God shall exalt thee on high; thou shalt triumph over all thy foes. Thy friends do stand by thee, and they shall hail thee again with warm hearts and friendly hands. Thou art not yet as

Job; thy friends do not contend against thee, neither charge thee with transgression, as they did Job." (D&C 121:7–10.)

The Lord then told Joseph what he will tell any of us in our loss, if we listen: "All these things shall give thee experience, and shall be for thy good." (D&C 122:7.) There is purpose in opposition, and no loss is so tragic and total that we cannot reclaim some good from it. Then the Lord gives us this great theological and psychological truth: "The Son of Man hath descended below them all. Art thou greater than he?" (D&C 122:8.) In ways that are incomprehensible to us, but nevertheless true, the Lord Jesus has suffered the accumulated load of all our losses. He has felt the pain and crippling of lost limbs, the frustration and helplessness of blindness, the isolation of deafness, the discouragement of hard work unrewarded, the bitterness of betrayal, the anguish of loved ones lost. He has consumed the bitterest of all life's fruits – the loss of virtue, opportunity, strength, and self-respect that comes when we sin. If all the lists like yours of all the people who ever lived, or ever will, were brought before him and all the blessings scribbled out so that humanity was almost a total loss and the weeping and wailing reached the heights of heaven and the depths of hell, it would not equal the sum of suffering that the Christ has endured for our sake.

Take a moment with your scribbled-out list in front of you to contemplate how much Jesus loves us – enough to have endured such loss and such suffering. Then realize that because of his love, and because we have not the strength or the calling he had, we have not been called upon to suffer the agony that he did. We are only called upon to suffer such deprivation as we can handle and as will be for our good. Therefore, we can begin to add back to our lists those things that have not been taken from us. Do that now. Take another sheet of paper and add back the things previously crossed out. As you list each one, stop and savor it. See your life become more rich and full with every blessing added back. My experience is that when you have completed your list, you will have a new appreciation for what you have left, and new strength and optimism to handle what you have lost.

Chapter 4

Manage Your Moods

. . . .

"It could have been so much worse. We were really blessed."
I have heard that expression all my life from my mother. She said
it many years ago when friends helped her back home from an
accident that totalled the car and banged up and bruised her, but
left everybody still alive. She said it when the kitchen caught fire
but didn't burn down the house. She said it when heart attacks
hit her as a young mother and might have left her an invalid, but
didn't. She said it later when the advancing years brought cataracts
to her eyes and pains and discomforts to her body. It is her theme
song: "We are so blessed; it could have been so much worse."

Some people just naturally choose to see the positive side of
a misfortune. There is an old country anecdote about a grandma
who always chose this response to difficulties. She was always
saying, "It could have been worse. It could have been worse."
Her grandchildren decided to see how far Grandma would really
go with this doctrine, so they concocted a story and ran to her
one day screaming, "Grandma, Grandma, something terrible has
happened! Cousin Jozy got carried off by the devil!"

Grandma said, of course, "Well, it could have been worse. It
could have been worse."

The children said, "Grandma, that's ridiculous. Cousin Jozy
was carried off by the devil. How could it have been worse?"

Grandma said, "The devil could have made Jozy carry him."

I didn't know the grandma in that story, but I know my own

mother well. She chose early in her life to take that stance in the face of misfortune. She got it from her own mother, who lost a twelve-year-old daughter to heart disease, watched a son in his thirties die of diabetes, and lived thirty-two years as a widow. My grandmother also, no matter what the trials, felt she was blessed, because "it could have been so much worse." My grandmother knew, and my mother knows, that those are not just idle words they toss off to try to look courageous in the face of adversity. They state a simple fact: things can always be worse than they are. By focusing on how bad things are *not*, these noble women are able to manage the moods that come to them in adversity. Words have a powerful effect to help us set our moods and the state of our heart and mind.

Music also has great power. Many years ago in Massachusetts, Elder Boyd K. Packer advised a group of us that when we are discouraged or downcast or tempted to do evil, we can think of our mind as a stage. Little actors come out on that stage to give our minds certain messages. If these are not the thoughts and feelings we want to hold, there is an easy way to sweep the stage and bring on better actors. "Just hum your favorite hymn," Elder Packer said, "and it will drive those bad actors off the stage of your mind and bring on the good actors."

I took his advice and chose my favorite hymn, and over the years I fancy I have become one of the great hummers of the Church. I thought at first that the process was too simple, almost a child's game. You may feel the same way. But after decades of experience, I can tell you that it's a very powerful tool in managing your moods. Several years before I got this helpful counsel from Elder Packer, I was the only American elder on the group of tiny islands in the little kingdom of Tonga in the South Pacific. Because of government restrictions at that time, we were only allowed three foreign proselyting missionaries in Tonga. Each of us had a local companion and lived among those wonderful people. But I was a long way from home for a long time. Sometimes I got homesick and lonely. I didn't know much about psychology or counseling, but I knew that sitting on the bow of those tiny ships plying the waters between the islands and singing my songs of home to the fish and the friendly waves surely made me feel better.

Music can match your mood and also help you change it. One of the most powerful ways to make this happen is by inviting music into your heart that matches your mood at first. If you are sad, feel free to sing, hum, whistle, or play on a phonograph or tape recorder sad songs that match your mood. Then, as the music begins to capture you, gradually change it to a brighter and brighter motif until it helps to pull you out of the doldrums. Any kind of good music will do — folk music, popular music, classical music — whatever music touches your heart and lifts it.

Several years ago a funeral was held for one of the beloved ladies in the Church, Jessie Evans Smith. She was the wife of President Joseph Fielding Smith. Her beautiful voice had inspired generations of Mormons and non-Mormons alike as she sang in the Tabernacle Choir and as a soloist. Her bubbling good humor was legendary, and the folk tales surrounding her made her probably the nearest thing we have to a female counterpart of J. Golden Kimball. If ever a beloved woman would be missed by the Saints, it was Jessie Evans Smith. The *Los Angeles Times* noted this in reporting her funeral. They also made note of the fact that there was not a sign of black in the entire Tabernacle. The Tabernacle Choir was dressed in beautiful colors; the room was festooned with flowers; the speakers were dressed in subdued and respectful tones, but not in somber shades. Sister Smith probably wanted it that way, and the President complied with her wishes. She had lived her life in happy colors and wanted to be remembered that way.

Color can do a lot for us in managing our moods. Reds, oranges, and other hot colors can arouse us. If we are feeling angry or stressed, they will add to that feeling. If we are deep in depression, they may help to bring us out. Many hospital rooms and doctors' gowns are pastel blue or green because this helps to calm patients who are under the stress of sickness or surgery. In times of pain or stress following a loss, you may want to choose carefully the colors that surround you and arrange them as much as possible to your benefit. It is a good way to help manage your moods.

We all know that a blue sky tends to brighten our outlook, and a gray, overcast one subdues it. The blue and gray skies contain more than just a difference of color. The clear sky allows the sunlight to penetrate to the world and into our lives. It is no coincidence that sunlight is so often used as a metaphor for happiness, brightness, and joy. Researchers are still looking into this, but already the indications are strong that sunlight itself can affect our moods. Many people get more subdued, even depressed, in the wintertime simply because the days are shorter, the nights are longer, and they have less sunlight around them. We may not realize how powerful sunlight is — probably because it is all around us.

Part of what I do for a living is to make video productions. I remember one scene we were shooting inside a room against a window. The window was on the north side, and there was no direct sunlight coming in. We masked the window with black plastic and turned on our inside lights to the fullest, but they were still no match for the outside light seeping in. Even bright artificial lighting has only a tiny fraction of the power of sunlight. It also does not contain all the wavelengths found in natural lighting. That is why plants grown under artificial lighting require special grow lights, which produce a wider spectrum of light. Lights similar to these can be obtained for home lighting, and they may help. You may also find that getting out in the sun when it is available helps to brighten your mood when you are down.

No factor of mood management is more powerful than the other people we associate with. Gary Dayton passes himself off as a barber at the Brigham Young University student center and at the Missionary Training Center in Provo, Utah. But he really is a counselor and a good-humor man. He gives good haircuts, no doubt about that, and a good haircut can brighten your life. But more than that, he has an infectious smile, a ready ear, a storyteller's skill, and a bottomless supply of anecdotes that have put a smile on his customers' faces for several decades now. I'm convinced that over the years many downcast souls have come in for a trim when they didn't want a haircut as badly as they wanted a word of encouragement. From my observation, our world is full of such dispensers of sunshine. Don't be afraid to call on them when you need help. They are people whom the Lord has blessed with a special talent for lifting others. They have developed that talent over the years, and will generally enjoy sharing it with us to our benefit. Usually, all they and the Lord will ask in return is that we ourselves help others later when we are stronger. As we absorb the sunshine from these saintly people, we find ourselves growing brighter. We tend to look for and bring out the brightness in others. We discover again that optimism and pessimism both tend to feed on themselves. They are like a breeder nuclear reactor. This power plant can, theoretically at least, create light and heat out of radioactive materials. When it finishes, it has created more fuel than it has consumed.

When we suffer a loss in our lives, one subtle side effect is a loss of confidence in our ability to control our own lives. We may say, with Job, "For the thing which I greatly feared is come upon me." (Job 3:25.) We may feel we are at the mercy of powers beyond our control. In a sense this is true, since few of us would voluntarily bring loss and pain upon ourselves. But we will be farther along in the healing process when we realize just how much of our destiny we still hold in our own hands. We cannot control all the things that happen to us, but we can in large measure control our response to them. By managing as much as we can such things as the words we say, the thoughts we think, the songs we sing and listen to, the colors about us, the amount of sunlight we absorb, the people we associate with, and other variables in our lives, we can in a great measure manage our moods. We can spend less time in the shadows of depression and more time in the sunshine of hope, and we will heal more quickly.

Chapter 5

Controlled Dreaming

. . . .

"I was never very big, but I always loved sports. I remember when I was ten I came home from a softball game grinning all over. My dad said, 'Did you win?' I said, 'No, we lost twenty-one to one.' My dad was a gruff man. He said, 'What are you smiling about, then?' I said, 'I was the one.' "

Sheila still wasn't very big in stature as she sat across the table from me. But she was tough enough to have endured a hard childhood, an abusive marriage, and a bitter divorce. As she told me about these and other experiences, I could see why she had survived. Her dark eyes sparkled and her face lit up when she relived in her memory the good times in her past. She savored them not only as happy reminiscences, but as raw material on which to build her dreams of the present and future.

History and the scriptures speak powerfully and repeatedly of the role that dreams have played in people's lives. The line of demarcation between dreams, visions, inspirations, daydreaming, meditation, and conscious imaging can be as hazy and blurred as the line between sleeping and wakefulness. Sometimes we snap out of a dead slumber into alert wakefulness. Other times we drift out of dreams slowly into a conscious awareness of our actual surroundings. Thus it is with the dreamlike states of the brain. If you are tucked under your covers, it is dark, your eyes are closed, you are unconscious to the world around you, but you are experiencing vivid scenes in your head, you can pretty well define that as a dream. If you are going through your daily routine and your mind wanders for a few seconds to another subject, that may be only reverie, memory, or idle thoughts. But between these two points is a continuum of mental activities that partake of aspects of the dreamlike state. They have several things in common. For one thing, the conscious awareness of the brain is relatively at rest. The brain actually emits a different shape of electromagnetic waves during these states. A second similarity of all these dream-like states is their powerful effect on our conscious mind and on our emotions. Dreams and meditations can trigger emotions, and vice versa.

We jokingly talk about nightmares being triggered by something we ate. That happens, of course, but more often our dreams are triggered by something we thought or felt before we went to sleep. I have often wakened, as I'm sure you have, from a bizarre dream and wondered what dark corner of my mind that sprang from. I cannot usually think of a visual picture to match the dream: in my daytime life, I rarely get chased by two-headed monsters or find myself downtown in my pajamas. But if I take a moment, I can usually match the emotion. If the dream was soothing and pleasant, I can think of similar feelings I had the night before, the day before, or within the past few days. If the dream was bitter or angry, I can often think of some real or imagined slight I suffered in the conscious world. If the dream was frightening, it usually traces back to feelings of insecurity I may have faced in my job or church calling or relationships with others. I find that feelings and emotions are like the scents in the nose of a bloodhound. You can't see them or describe them exactly, but they are fairly easy to trace and to recognize when you feel them again.

Recognizing this tie of dreams and dreamlike mental states to feelings is important as we learn to overcome our losses. It is even more important that we develop the power to control these dreams and the effects they have on our feelings, at least in a measure. Emotions and feelings are where we really live. Our outward environment may be palatial or poverty-stricken, our physical appearance handsome or homely, our state of health robust or precarious, our circle of friends large or small—but none of these is anywhere nearly as important to our happiness as are our feelings and emotions. When we control them, we control our joy and our destiny.

One effective tool for adjusting our mental and emotional conditions is a technique called controlled dreaming. The aim of controlled dreaming is to gain access to the powerful communication channels into the unconscious mind, which open during states of relaxation, reverie, and sleep. During these times the watchdog of the conscious mind is lulled temporarily off guard. This is important, because normally this useful but sometimes meddlesome mutt tries to intervene between us and our unconscious mind. He barks, yaps, snaps, and tries to drive away any messages that don't seem to be in accordance with his view of reality. So when we tell ourselves, "I can be happy despite my difficulties; I can turn this obstacle into a stepping stone and come back stronger than I was before," the conscious-mind watchdog leaps barking between us and our goal. He yaps and snarls and whines messages such as these: "This is a terrible loss; you will never recover. No one in history ever suffered as much as you are suffering now. You deserve to be down and discouraged after what the world (or the Lord) has done to you. It's a Pollyanna fairy tale to try to make this loss anything less than it is. The real situation is this." He then describes things in the worst way, and our strengths as weak as we can picture them, and calls that an objective view of the world.

One of Satan's most powerful tools is fear. He digs a mighty chasm between us and the healed person we would hope to become. Then he throws us over the edge and dangles us by the thin strands of hope as he taunts us with the terrible "what-ifs": What if things get even worse than they are now? What if this loss is just the beginning of a landslide of catastrophes upon me? What if my strength fails? What if I grow too old to handle it? What if I cave in? What if I slip into a depression and never come out? He has a million of these, each one finely tuned to our own particular weaknesses and each one designed to pluck out a thread from our lifeline of hope.

Does this mean that our conscious mind is the devil's advocate, our opponent in the struggle—that we have actually turned upon ourselves? It doesn't seem reasonable that we would deliberately try to defeat our own cause, but the answer to the question is yes. We ourselves are the yapping, snapping, junkyard dog standing between us and the better world we would aspire to. For reasons that are not clear to psychologists, theologians, or even to ourselves, we often deliberately choose darkness rather than light, pain rather than joy. We often reopen and let fester our own emotional wounds rather than helping them to heal, or at least letting them alone so they can begin to heal by themselves. No one knows all the reasons why we do this, but we do.

The quickest recovery would be, of course, to muzzle our personal "hound of the Baskervilles," shove him into his dog-house, and nail the door shut. That's fine when it works, but often we have fed, groomed, and trained this brute until he is now more powerful than we are. In a fight with him we always lose. We tell ourselves, "Hey, I can feel better tomorrow," or "I can overcome this loss," or "I can win this time." We think we are doing fine, but then we lose or fail and drop back into depression. Late that night we hear an echo from the doghouse of our mind saying, "I thought I could, but I knew I couldn't." The double-crossing watchdog of the conscious mind chuckles softly as he digs a hole and buries another of our aspirations.

So what can we do? If we can't be stronger than the watchdog is, we must be smarter. We must wait until he's asleep, then slip past him and tiptoe on toward the brighter world of our healed selves. Unfortunately, he doesn't sleep as often as we wish he would. When he does, we're too groggy to do anything about it. Controlled dreaming is a technique designed to lull the conscious mind to sleep, or at least into fairly passive resistance. Then we can get our message through to the unconscious mind, which can change our outlook and thereby change our world.

The technique is simple, but very powerful. Find yourself a

quiet spot, sit down in a comfortable chair with your feet flat on the floor, or even lie down. (Don't try to do this when you are exhausted or you will go into an uncontrolled dream and wake up late for an appointment.) While you are conscious, close your eyes and concentrate on relaxing every muscle in your body. There are techniques for doing this. One of the easiest is simply to focus on groups of muscles, starting in your chest and then working down to your abdomen, hips, upper legs, lower legs, feet, toes — then into your shoulders and up into your head and face, then into your upper arm muscles, lower arm muscles, and finally your fingers. As you focus on each one of these muscle groups, deliberately tighten them for three seconds; then relax. You will feel them let go.

After you have gone through your entire body, feel if there are any unrelaxed muscles. If so, merely repeat the technique on them. You are now relaxed. Your brain is functioning somewhat on the sleep-wave cycle. In this mode, your brain will take suggestions and carry them more effectively to your unconscious mind. It will respond to words, music, smells, and visual images, but one of the most effective communication devices is mental pictures. Start the film of your life as you would like it to be, with wide-screen panoramic vision, quadraphonic sound, and all the special effects you want. Make it as real as you can. See yourself in the situations that now trouble you. See yourself overcoming them and putting them past you. See yourself in the situation that you would like to be in.

Uh oh, a bad scene. You tried to leap over a hurdle, caught your toe, and fell flat on your face on the track. So much for that movie, right? Wrong. It's your movie. You own the copyrights, the film footage, the editing equipment, the projection equipment, the theater, the seat, and even the popcorn. You can do whatever you want to in your movie, so stop the film, rewind, and splice in a new scene. In this scene you clear that hurdle magnificently and go on to the next one. If you trip again, stop the movie, snip out the scene, and edit it again until finally the negative part of you will give up. You will clear that hurdle in your movie and move on. At first you may tire out in ten minutes or so. Later you will be able to go for a half hour or more. Like any mental or physical skill, the more you do it the better at it you will get. But even the first time through, you will probably have helpful results—even if you open your eyes, stand up, and return immediately to the sad world you left. For those few moments, you have lived in the world of your dreams. Your watchdog will probably wake up barking and bellowing, but it is too late. You have slipped a message of hope past him, and the unconscious mind—the control center of your real world—has received it and recognized it.

Do this again and again. As you do so, your messages will get stronger and your movie more positive. In the process your conscious-mind watchdog will begin to turn from a snarling adversary into a tongue-lapping, tail-wagging ally. That is an important point. We were a little hard on the conscious mind just now. Actually, the conscious mind is not our natural enemy, but neither is he our natural friend. He is a powerful force for good or ill; we decide which. And in those first hard days and weeks after a loss, we need all the friends we can get.

Traveling Tips

. . . .

Following is a list of mental and physical activities to help you along the journey thus far. They will be useful anytime you are down, but they are designed specifically for combatting the first shock waves that accompany your loss:

Pamper yourself a little. Physically, mentally, and emotionally you probably won't have as much to give because your strength in these areas is being siphoned off to work through the shock to your system. It isn't self-pity or self-indulgence to lighten up your loads in other areas a bit. You are saving your resources to apply to recuperating from your loss and to being more effective in the future. Usually friends, family, and fellow workers will understand this and be considerate.

Eat the right things, even though you may not have much of an appetite. A balanced, nourishing diet is important here. You may even consider a food supplement for a time to make sure your body is receiving the nutrition to work through this difficult process.

Cry if you need to. We sometimes develop the opinion that crying is for sissies, and big people don't do it. But big people do cry, in various ways and for various reasons. If crying seems to help release the pressure bottled up within you, then find a quiet place and cry.

Go ahead and think about your loss. We sometimes feel we have to get our minds off our loss. Eventually we do, of course, but our minds are naturally curious and inquisitive. If we try to lock them out of this part of our lives, they will constantly sniff and poke around it. Like forbidden fruit, the subject will tempt and tantalize our minds, and the more we tell ourselves, "I shouldn't think about this," the more we will tend to think about it. The easiest way to guarantee that our minds will hover on a subject is to command them that they shouldn't. But if the mind is given full rein to ponder and consider and reenact even the most painful parts of our loss, after a while our curiosity is fulfilled, the subject loses its intrigue, and the mind naturally goes on to other things. This moving on is a sign of healing.

Use the powerful imaging abilities of your "right brain," but use them gently. During the past few years researchers have gained a new appreciation for the mind's abilities to picture and create vivid scenes. These images tend to pull our thoughts and our actions in certain directions. Right now, you are hurting and in a kind of shock. It may be too much to ask of your system to rally its forces and carry on as though nothing had happened. Your thoughts are slower, and sometimes foggy. Your judgments may be clouded. Your energy level is down. You probably don't want to take on any ambitious projects at this time. But even in this subdued state, your mind will always be active. If left to itself it may lead you into depressing scenes and frightening possibilities. It may picture you unable to cope with coming challenges — this loss triggering additional losses, helplessness, and hopelessness. But with a little gentle leading, you can coach your mind into picturing happier scenarios for you. Gently daydream about the situations in which you would like to see yourself. Don't be depressed if many or most of these situations seem to be replays of the time before your loss. That's natural. As time passes, your mind will find ways of adapting your present situation nearer to the happy scenes before your loss. It's one of the incredible powers of your imagination. But even as that is happening, these fantasies can bring warmth to your soul and can even help your physical system to work better. So go ahead and dream of things as you would like them to be.

Let others help you. One of the reimbursements paid you for your loss is often a greater appreciation for how much milk of human kindness is flowing through society. There is, of course, much hardheartedness in the world. But when you need help, as you now do, it will likely surprise you how many people pop up and want to be counted as your friends.

Keep breathing. Stay alive. You may not want to. A desire for death is a very natural feeling after a great loss. Simply surviving from day to day is a victory in your present state, and you should consider it so. Every breath you take, every moment that passes is a tiny score for your side. Every passing moment leaves behind a thin layer of the balm of Gilead to soothe your troubled soul and to help heal the open wound brought on by your loss. As you survive, little by little you will overcome.

Keep moving. Move at a gentle and reduced pace, but move nevertheless.

Do more of the things you want to do. Don't be disappointed if they don't hold the same zest they had at other times. That is natural in your present state. But take what joy and interest and involvement you can from them.

Read and ponder the scriptures and the words of the prophets. Nothing gives us perspective on our losses as the scriptures do. Here we find the purpose and the plan of our lives. We see that no loss is permanent. We understand some of the reasons why loss is a vital part of the plan. Other writers may console us. They may give us new insights and ideas. These are valuable, but the scriptures are the sure word of the Lord. The word of God is the iron rod to which we can hold as we work our way through the fog of our present crisis and continue our journey back to the presence of God.

Meditate and pray. One member of the Eternal Godhead has the specific responsibility to care for you in times such as these. This is the Holy Ghost. He is, among other things, a comforter. His influence can touch your heart and your mind. He can soothe your pains and stanch the emotional hemorrhaging that is draining your strength. He is also assigned to bring to you knowledge, "even hidden treasures" of knowledge. This knowledge can include glimpses of better times coming for you, ideas on how to endure your present hard situation, and visions of eternity that can help you put your loss into perspective. A time of loss is an excellent opportunity to draw on the powers of this omnipotent God who stands ready to help you. One of the best ways to tap these powers is through prayer and meditation. These times can be spiritual oases dotting the desert of your present existence. You will do well to drink from them and use their strength to help you move into the greener valleys beyond this arid place you are now struggling through.

Part 2

The Long,
Gray Grind

Milestone Markers

As we discussed at the beginning of the first stage, overcoming your loss is a journey. As you move into the next stage of your journey, you may feel there are attitudes and attributes in the first stage that you still need to work on. Don't let them concern you. You can review that section whenever you need to, but for now, move into this next section to give yourself a better overall view of the journey you are making.

When we sustain a serious loss in our lives, the second phase toward recovery often involves what I have called here "the long, gray grind." The initial shock and grief of the loss have worn off. The outpourings of condolence and support have slowed to a small stream or a trickle, or have stopped altogether. This is fine. It is uncomfortable and unhealthy to be the focus of others' concerns for too long. The jarring changes in our life patterns have largely been made. Now it is time to learn to live with the loss.

This segment of the healing process usually comes on more gradually and lasts longer than the first painful phase. It is a condition we need to initiate at least partly by ourselves. The initial loss was thrust upon us, and we had little or no control over when or how it would happen. This second period will likewise gradually come as a matter of course, but we can adjust the timing by our mental and emotional set. This phase is vital to the healing process. It is important that we experience it and that we work directly through it. To try to avoid this part of the grief process would only slow our recovery, because sooner or later we must face the realities of our situation. Then we must adjust to our new lifestyle and develop the strength to live in the world that is now given to us. The mental and emotional attributes we want to achieve on this part of our journey have to do with adjusting to the long-term effects of our loss. Sooner or later, we want to be able to make these statements and believe them in our inner heart and soul:

I have looked unflinchingly into the face of my present situation; there is no pain or sorrow there that I have tried to hide from.

On the other hand, I have not exaggerated my loss to make it more than it really is.

I am committed to go on living to the fullest extent possible despite my loss.

I am learning to use the wisdom I gained from my loss to empathize with and help others through their pain.

Every day I am gaining a little more strength to overcome my loss.

I gain strength and confidence to face the future as I look back at what I have endured already.

I am using the insights gained from my loss to better understand the eternal purposes of God for his children, and particularly for me. I can begin to see the light at the end of my tunnel of grief, or at least to believe that such light is possible.

I am beginning to smile again and to look forward and enjoy some aspects of my life, even when they remind me of my loss.

Though I will always remember my loss, it will become a gentle memory to me—not a stabbing pain or an aching depression.

Chapter 6

Time on Your Hands
or by Your Side

· ·

"Call me Charlie," he says, and almost everybody complies with his wishes. When you are seventeen and your thoughts, your ideas, your conversations haven't fully matured, Charlie is an appropriate and youthful name. The only problem is that Charlie is not seventeen anymore, except in parts of his mind and his emotions. His unsympathetic birth certificate says he is nearing the age of retirement, but parts of Charlie are stuck back there on that fateful day when he was seventeen and his brother was killed in a car accident. Charlie never learned how to deal with the grief and guilt of it all. The accident wasn't his fault. People have tried to tell him that over the years, and he nods in agreement. But deep down inside him somewhere, something snapped that day and has never been reconnected. He's a fairly normal human being. He's not paranoid or schizophrenic, but he is a little eccentric because, apparently, he has never learned to deal with the grief of the loss of his brother. Part of him wants to live in the time before that loss and refuses to budge much beyond it.

In the days of Charlie's loss, not much was known about grief therapy. There is still a great deal to learn, but one truth is apparent: we must work through our feelings of grief and loss. If we don't, the mere passage of time will not necessarily help us. In Charlie's case, he has immunized himself against the soothing effects of the balm of time. In fact, in those areas of his life most affected by the loss of his brother, time appears to have stopped.

He talks a great deal about his brother and about the things they did together. There is nothing wrong with remembering, of course, but when Charlie talks you get the feeling it happened the day before yesterday. And sadder than this, you get the feeling that nothing worth remembering has happened since then. Few, if any, joyful experiences or growing, maturing events seem to have occurred in Charlie's life since that great loss. It is apparent that time cannot help us overcome our losses if we do not allow it to pass.

I got the same feeling from the famous cartoonist Al Capp. During his heyday in the forties and fifties, his cartoon "L'il Abner" was probably the most popular comic strip in America. His characters of Mammy Yokum, Daisy Mae, Marryin' Sam, Senator Fogbound, and others were practically members of millions of American families. A few weeks ago our high school kids got dressed up and went to a Sadie Hawkins Day dance at their school. It was an occasion where the girls asked the boys for a date. They had the idea of the affair, but had no idea who Sadie Hawkins was. So I told them about the famous unmarriageable daughter in Dogpatch, U.S.A., L'il Abner's hometown. Every year her father would stage the Sadie Hawkins Day race in which the panicky, eligible bachelors would run for their unmarried lives, pursued hotly by Sadie and any other of the unmarriageable maidens who wanted to participate. Sadie's father cheered her on with these encouraging words, "Go out and catch a husband, or I may have you on my hands for the rest of my natural life." It was great fun in its day, but obviously would not be considered very funny anymore. The idea of single women frantically pursuing bachelors as their only source of happiness, temporal salvation, and self-worth is not an idea that brings smiles to the lips of many women and women's organizations today.

The point is that times changed and Al Capp lost popularity. Frankly, he didn't take it too well. In his later years he became negative and sarcastic and really wasn't very funny. It seemed he did not progress to the next stage of his life, which time and the changes of society presented to him. So he magnified his loss and turned it from a loss of public popularity with his present way of doing things to a personal affront, a betrayal from his formerly loyal public. That brought an end to his delightful cartooning.

Time, at least in our present human condition, is designed to pass inexorably. It refuses to stop, no matter what our pleadings. It does not respond to the command of the mightiest potentate. It moves. There will come a time, apparently, when this condition will not exist. The Apostle John saw in vision a day when "there should be time no longer." (Revelation 10:6.) But for now, time continues to tick, and there is nothing we can do to stop it. I believe this principle illustrates again the benevolence and condescension of God toward us as children. In that day when time will stop, sorrow, pain, death, and loss will already have been conquered. Eternal bliss will be our status. At that point, our merciful Father will apparently stop time and allow us to dwell in those celestial conditions forever.

Until that blessed day, who of us would want to stop time? If we did so, we would all be literally damned—stopped in our progress, unable to improve, repent, and heal from our losses. So for now, time continues to flow as a relentless river. How can we catch the flow and sail smoothly with it instead of defeating ourselves by paddling against the current? Among other things, we need to keep time by our side and not on our hands.

When we suffer a loss, we enter into a fascinating love/hate relationship with time. Time is our ally and our adversary, our friend and our foe. As the realization of our loss first closes in upon us, time stops. It allows us to sit and suffer in limbo. Hours and days may pass for others, but not for us. It is always the same time—the time of tragedy. Appointments are unimportant. Even the demands of hunger, thirst, and sleep are filled only cursorily and automatically, and sometimes ignored altogether. We go through the motions of being in sync with the rest of the world, but inside the clock has stopped ticking and the calendar has stopped turning its pages.

Time is on our hands; it is a dead weight on our heart and mind. Sometimes we make the mistake of solidifying this relationship because of pain, heartache, and disappointment. We try to stop time. We try to petrify and embalm it at some period before this great loss and hurt came upon us.

Some parents who have lost a child lock the door to the little one's room and never change an article inside. Some older people who have experienced the natural but sometimes painful loss of youth never quite get over it. They choose to dress and behave as they did decades earlier. They have their faces and their tummies lifted. They frantically try to deny the passage of time. They see it as only a loss of their youth.

Some people who have lost material resources try to freeze time in the period when they still had abundance, by continuing to live a lifestyle beyond their means. In so doing they often waste precious resources that could help them fight back from their financial loss.

It is a natural thing to want to turn back the clock and stop its hands at the moment before we suffered our loss. But it is, of course, a frustrating exercise in uselessness. Time refuses to stop, and we are fortunate that it does. It is fitting and proper to memorialize, remember, and commemorate the loss of those we love. It is appropriate and invigorating to think young thoughts and remain active as one grows older. It is often motivating when one loses material things to remember good times and strive appropriately to overcome adversity and return to comfort and even prosperity. But these are different from frantic attempts to freeze time in its tracks. When we try to stop time, we do not memorialize the dead as we continue on living. We cut ourselves off from any future joys and live only in the rewarmed memories of yesterday. When we frantically try to capture and hold onto youth forever, we may make ourselves look eccentric or ridiculous, and we miss the warm and golden moments that come with maturity and even with old age.

When we deny the loss of status, position, or material means, we shut out the growth and new experiences that may come with struggle. I have known men who could not accept being released from church callings. They continued to live as though they were in their previous position of authority, which caused problems for themselves and for those who succeeded them. I knew a family once in the South Seas who had struggled mightily to keep their branch of the Church together. They were the entire Church organization on their island. Eventually, government restrictions were lifted, others joined the Church, and the branch began to flourish. New leaders were called, and members of this family were released with a vote of thanks. It would have been a fine experience for them to accept their new role and enjoy the growth of others about them, but they instead chose to freeze history in the period when they were most important. They left the Church and lived in the past in their own organization where they were still the leaders.

If we try to stop time, it will turn on us as an adversary. It may boldly attack us with new losses and new tragedies. But more likely it will oppose us in slow, quiet, and subversive ways. It will detach us from reality and force us to live in the past, in the days when we had our loved one or loved things. As memory fades, we will substitute fantasies and make our past lives more and more beautiful. By comparison, our present days will seem more and more dismal and gray. If we have lost a spouse, he or she will get to be so wonderful in our own mind that no living person could ever share our life, being so far short of the person we had been married to before. The story is told of a preacher who stood before his congregation to make a point about forgiveness, and he said, "All of you who are perfect, please stand." To his surprise a man in the back row stood up. The preacher said, "Brother, are you telling us that you are perfect?" The man said, "No, I'm standing here as proxy for my wife's first husband." I suspect that first husband got more perfect every day in his wife's memory.

Time will play these tricks on us if we try to bottle it up and screw the lid down. It will seep out the cracks. It will ooze through our defenses. It will distort our present and dim our future. On the other hand, if we can bring ourselves to look beneath time's doleful, brooding, unfriendly face in our moment of loss, we will see a friend sitting deep inside. This is not an easy or a natural thing to do. We must lift ourselves by force of will and make ourselves take time's hand and walk with him along the rocky trail of our lives. The first steps will definitely be uphill. The path will be rough; the stones will cut our feet. The sun will be too hot, and the wind will be too cold. The unknown country beyond the next bend will frighten us, and we will doubt that we have the strength to make the grade. At times we will have only enough strength to take one step, breathe hard, gather our energies, and take another small, shuffling step.

As we move forward, we find that time not only becomes kind, but it also becomes one of the best friends we have. Its claws sunk into our hearts turn to gentle fingers that massage away the pain. Its steely grip holding us fast in our moment of loss turns to an inviting hand leading us away from our tragic moments and into an unexplored future. Its brooding brow staring on us softens and shows a twinkle of promise in the eyes. Even if events continue to rain down tragedy and loss upon us, time will stand by our side if we will let it. The story is told of an oriental potentate who had everything his heart could desire until his heart's desire was taken from him: his beloved daughter died. He was inconsolable and offered a rich reward to any who could free him from the icy grip of grief. The wise man who eventually claimed the prize gave the great potentate a ring and told him to wear it always and read the inscription often. The simple words were, "This, too, shall pass."

Time makes us that promise always, even if the future should turn out to be more loss and greater grief. The whispered promise from our friend Time is that "this, too, shall pass." Brigham Young sang to his Saints in their hard times during the first years in the Salt Lake Valley, "Hard times, hard times, come again no more. Many days you have lingered around our cabin door. But now we've brighter days in store."

There will be brighter days in store. If the brighter days are postponed even until the next world, so be it. The promise is still sure that we are not locked forever in the grip of the present tragic moment of loss.

Chapter 7

Making the Body
Move the Mind

Traditionally, in history and literature, great battles begin at dawn. But Anne Karren prefers to get the jump on the enemy. She marshals her forces even before the first gray streaks light the eastern sky. She will not win the war on this or any other day, but her single-handed holding action may keep the enemy at bay. That is goal enough for her fighting spirit. The enemy is arthritis, and it grips her joints every night while she is asleep and has to be fought off every morning. Drugs and painkillers can help somewhat in the battle against this cruel crippler, but Anne prefers to engage him in hand-to-hand combat. And she usually wins that day's skirmish.

The alarm clock sounds the bell for another round in the battle. She fights her way through the fog of sleep and the great temptation that we all have just to lie there and let life take its course. Her first movements are met with stabs of pain. She pushes through them, gets up, dresses, and goes somewhat stiffly out the door to the street. Here she is met by a couple of other supportive sisters, and the little group walks from one streetlight to the next. They exercise not only their bodies but their minds as they discuss current events, philosophies, personal development, and gospel principles. By the end of the walk, Anne has at least got the edge on her adversary for the day. If she keeps busy in mind and body until bedtime, she usually keeps the upper hand. There is never a dearth of things to do in her busy life as wife, mother, and ward Relief Society president.

You might expect such a warrior woman to be steely eyed, heavy jawed, and built like an Amazon. Not so. Anne's eyes twinkle with life and humor. Her petite face still has the graceful lines of girlhood, and her trim figure belies the fact that she is a grandmother. Gently, personally, on a darkened battlefield of the street, and within the quiet confines of her own heart and mind, Anne Karren is the quintessential happy warrior. She has lost what most of us consider a satisfying sensory experience—lounging in a lazy body. But in exchange she has developed a rare ability to use her body to control her mind and emotions.

One of the fundamental purposes for which we came to this world was to gain a body. We often say that, but we don't often say why. Why would we want to clothe our free and immortal spirits in flesh and bone subject to temptation, disease, and, in a short time, death and decay? Eventually, of course, our bodies will rise again, glorified, resurrected, and eternal—that will solve all the problems we are discussing in this book. But we are dealing with the here and now. In our present circumstances we have bodies that can be a burden, but they can also be a marvelous blessing.

I believe that we needed and wanted a body—despite its inherent limitations in its present state—because the body gives us access to our spirits in a way that nothing else can. The body is strung together with what we call voluntary muscles. They may not be as voluntary as we would like. They sometimes won't move as quickly, effectively, or smoothly as we would like them to. They sometimes sag and bag, but as a general rule they do respond to the electrical impulses we send out from our brain. These movements are ultimately the best access we have to reach the spirit inside us. That, I believe, is the most important reason for having a body.

It is obvious that the most talented, hard-working, dedicated, well-organized, task-oriented, management-by-objectives person who ever lived will not accomplish very much in this life. At best we live a few short years, build a few buildings, create a few works of art, or plow some fields. We may be lucky and end up as head of a great corporation, or even be born a king. But we won't accomplish a great deal toward changing the shape or destiny of the world. We delude ourselves if we think we will. Percy Bysshe Shelley's poem "Ozymandias" is the most eloquent, succinct summation I know of this truth. Shelley writes of a traveler who describes an inscription near what had once been a magnificent statue: "My name is Ozymandias, King of Kings: Look on my works, ye Mighty, and despair!" But all around the statue, "The lone and level sands stretch far away."

I once visited a display of the greatest artifacts from a man about whom "Ozymandias" could have been written, Ramses the Great, Pharaoh of Egypt. Among other reasons, Ramses' reputation was great because he went around scraping off the names of previous Pharaohs and inscribing his own on their works. Still, in his day he was king of kings. In our day he is a traveling museum show of little brass trinkets and hunks of carved granite.

The point is that none of us can accumulate enough accomplishments to change mankind or to buy our way into heaven. Why work, then? Because it is the only way to reach inside our body where the spirit dwells and change the nature of our character. What the body does affects the mind, the spirit, and the character. This is vital information to know when our minds and spirits are in the rut of loss and depression. If we don't move them, they will stay there.

There used to be a sign on the long Alcan Highway stretching through the open spaces of Canada on to Alaska. The term *highway* was an overly generous one for this rutted dirt trail that was barely passable. Over the years, vehicles had worn down two deep tracks going each way. Once you were in those, it was hard to get out before you got to Alaska, so a humorous but wise sign at the head of the trail said, "Choose your ruts carefully; you're going to be in them for a long time."

Better advice for our travel down the road of life could not be given. After a loss we sometimes find ourselves dropped into ruts of grief and bereavement. If we don't move ourselves out of them, we can be in them for a long time—sometimes for the rest of our lives. This is where the body and the voluntary muscles come in handy. We need to take command of our bodies in these junctures because they will not be still. They will be moving in one direction or another. If we do not move them upward, they will dissipate downward. A body without motive power and moral direction will not remain stagnant or drift aimlessly. It will begin to sink under the pull of spiritual gravity that surrounds us all the time. Or it may be sucked down the vortex of sin or descend into depression.

Anthony Robbins, a well-known business and personal consultant, asks depressed people who come to him, "What do you do to get yourself into depression?" This is a surprising and sometimes offensive remark to these troubled souls. But Robbins is not placing blame. He is trying to follow a track so they can retrace their steps. He is right. Depression may be triggered by a loss, by a chemical imbalance in the brain, or by mental or emotional stimuli. There are any number of sources and reasons for depression. No one is minimizing the seriousness of those reasons, but depression is not like losing an arm or having your heart stop. Depression is brought on and maintained by certain physical actions—such things as looking down instead of looking up, lying in bed instead of getting up, using our energies to serve ourselves instead of other people. Again, this is not faultfinding or blaming the depressed person. He or she is often laboring under heavy burdens. This is just to say that those actions perpetuate and intensify depression, and the opposite physical actions tend to dispel the depression. So if we want to overcome the pain and grief that loss brings to us, one avenue is by the way we manipulate the voluntary muscles in our bodies. Here are some simple but effective things we can do.

Focus your attention on the facial muscles approximately an inch and a half to two inches on either side of your nose. Tighten these muscles gently. You will find a universal law of physiology. The body is supported by the tension of opposing muscle groups. The rule on which they operate is that when the muscles pulling in one direction apply pressure, the muscles in the other direction relax. (Parenthetically, this is one way to get rid of lordosis, sway back, and lower back pains – keep a stiff abdomen.) You will now feel this opposite pulling syndrome in the muscles of your cheeks. There will be resistance at first, but as you continue to send electrical signals to the upward-pulling muscle group, they will respond and the downward-pulling muscle group will relax. You will have created one of mankind's little miracles. You have now made the only universal sign that anthropologists have found in all their studies. Other hand and body signals and facial gestures vary from culture to culture. But the gesture you have just created is recognized throughout the earth as a sign of positive feelings, friendliness, love, and kindness. It is called a smile.

A smile projects good feelings outward to anyone who sees it. The research is quite definitive in this. What is less appreciated is the message that a smile projects inward. Among other things, manipulating the face in this configuration helps open up the blood vessels to the brain. A frown or a grimace constricts those same blood vessels. As the blood vessels open with a smile, more blood circulates into the brain and raises the brain's temperature. The brain responds by releasing chemicals that are natural pain relievers, stress reducers, and mellowing catalysts. They are mild forms of the deadly drugs that addicts get hooked on, but they are naturally produced and gently administered to answer our needs without developing unnatural cravings. A smile helps produce a natural and gentle high.

Another simple action we can take is to raise our eyes. Our biggest challenge in overcoming loss, I believe, is to lengthen our perspective, figuratively and literally. It is no accident that a down-cast look is associated with discouragement. That is the natural move for the body to make. It is our way of protecting ourselves when we feel we are vulnerable. When we look down, we are in a sense drawing our wagons into a circle, consolidating our resources, hiding out and holding on as we wait for the next attack to come. Every muscle contracts when it is in pain. Our eyes and our outlook do the same thing. We may need this protective device for a short time, but very soon we need to break out of this self-enclosed psychological shell in which we are hiding. One of the best ways to do that is to force the eyes up and out and lift the head. There is deep psychological as well as religious significance in Psalm 121:1, "I will lift up mine eyes unto the hills, from whence cometh my help." It is hard to focus your eyes on the farthest horizon, to climb to high points and look out, and still maintain the same closed-in perspective.

The reason perspective is so important is that it is ultimately the only answer to loss. When I lost my first wife, I had (and still have) a deep and abiding faith in the eternal nature of human beings. I knew of a certainty that I would see her again after this life. But my problem was to get through the years, the months, and the days that separated us. Focusing my eyes on the long view, the eternal perspective, helped me to keep from making an eternity out of the given grieving moment.

The spine and shoulders are likewise avenues of escape from the ruts of depression. Again, it is not by accident that folklore, literature, and scripture have focused on the back and the shoulders to symbolize the loads that we carry through life. The leg muscles are actually our strongest, and any professional athlete knows that they are the most important part of his performance (and, unfortunately, often the first to go as he ages). Mickey Mantle, the great home-run hitter, still had the arms and shoulders to punch a baseball out of the park. Joe Namath still had that howitzer of an arm that could fire a football sixty yards downfield. But both of them were finished when their knees gave out. We never say, "He carries a heavy load on his thighs." It is the "back-breaking labor" and "shouldering the burden" that immediately give us the image of life's heavy loads upon us. The reason we emphasize spine and shoulders is that when they are bent we are burdened. But when we stand tall with our shoulders thrown back and our spines held relatively straight, we are more in command of our environment. We can control this outlook through the application of our voluntary muscles.

The larynx is likewise controlled by voluntary muscles, as are the rib cage and the abdomen. When we contract our abdominal muscles, we force air through the folds of the voice box, which vibrate to make a basic sound. This sound is echoed through our nasal and facial cavities. It even reverberates through the bones of our head and face. The sound is molded by the tongue, the teeth, and the soft palate as it flows out of the mouth. The combination of these unique characteristics creates your individual voice and mine. It is a simple matter with most of us to constrict or relax these vocal folds. The result is a raising or lowering of the voice. With a bit of training we can adjust the resonance and the placement of the sound, which can change a growling, guttural voice or a whining twang into sweet and melodious music. These simple, voluntary changes in the way we speak can have dramatic effects on those about us and upon ourselves.

In Proverbs 15:1 we read, "A soft answer turneth away wrath." In our house of fifteen children, this counsel has been invaluable. Try this simple experiment: next time you answer the phone, have your voice go down at the end of the word *hello*. See what kind of effect this has on the person at the other end of the line. Chances are, he or she will be looking to hang up the receiver as soon as possible. Now put an upward turn on your greeting. This is an invitation to continue the conversation, a welcome into the world on your end of the phone line.

There are other, more complicated, voluntary actions we can take, and should take, with other parts of our body. Our legs and feet can carry us to settings that do not constantly remind us of our loss. Our hands can be busily engaged in the service of others. Our eyes can focus on roses and not thorns. Our ears can open to the laughter of children, the song of birds. Our noses can smell the flowers along life's path. These are subjects for another discussion, but even the simple things we have talked about here are very powerful. I guarantee that if you do them you will feel better, and you will overcome the adverse effects of your loss more quickly.

Chapter 8

Restructuring Reality
around Your Handicaps

· ·

A few years ago a policeman in a Midwestern city pulled over
to inspect what appeared to be a late-night larceny. A car was
parked at the curb in the darkness, and a man was underneath,
busily engaged with wrenches. The officer stopped his car and
demanded in the name of the law that the suspicious midnight
mechanic come out from under the car and explain his actions.

Iliff Jeffrey obligingly did so. It wasn't the first time he had
surprised the sighted world with his initiative and independence.
He was reared among southern Utah farmers whose creed of life
included pulling your own weight as much as possible and looking
for opportunities instead of excuses. His parents wisely chose not
to make an exception in their philosophy for three-year-old Iliff,
even though he had been blinded in an accident. He grew up
believing he could, should, and would develop his talents and do
his part to make the world better, and he did. He shared the chores
of the farm, later wrestled on his high school and college varsity
teams, and learned to play the guitar for recreation. He used this
and his other talents to woo a beautiful young woman for his
wife. He reared a fine family and was later named the most successful graduate of his high school class.

When he met up with the policeman that night, the future
Dr. Jeffrey was a struggling young medical student trying to save
a few dollars by doing his own mechanical work on his car. He
had learned to do this sort of thing, as every farmer does, by helping

to keep the farm machinery repaired on the family homestead. He explained to the officer that he often worked late at night since he was busy with classes and studying during the day. He had no need of a flashlight under the car because he had trained his fingers to see for him. The officer shook his head in amazement, as friends and acquaintances of Dr. Jeffrey have shaken their heads all his life. He hopped in his patrol car and drove away. The midnight mechanic went nonchalantly back to work.

Iliff Jeffrey was gentle in his explanation to the policeman. He is a gentle man, and his healing hands have blessed the lives of thousands over the course of a long career. He might have had a chuckle or two at the officer's expense. He might have said something like this, "I'm not using a light because I'm not handicapped, like you folks are. Your hands are so clumsy and your ears and other senses are so dull that you can't work in the dark like I can." That sounds a little cocky, so I'm sure Dr. Jeffrey would never use that approach. But in the world that he has made for himself, it is true.

In sharing the experiences of admirable handicapped people and this philosophy of restructuring your world to overcome handicaps, I certainly don't mean to imply that this is easy or natural. I would not minimize the difficulties that come with physical handicaps or the strength of character it takes to overcome them. I do not pretend to have personal insight into this difficult and discouraging form of loss in our lives. But from my observation, this is the path that those remarkable people have trod who have overcome their physical handicaps. They have found ways to restructure their world so that they could go on living and contributing to the good of others. In the process, they have made their own lives sweeter and have inspired the rest of us to do better with the physical abilities we have. But it is certainly not easy to do what they have done.

A prominent government official in England centuries ago gave us the true measure of a person's worth and the value of his work in the eternal perspective of things. John Milton had a promising career ahead of him until he went blind. He agonized over the loss of his opportunities. At length he picked up his pen and turned his talents to the subject that obsessed him. He left a poem of wisdom, "On His Blindness," that has lived longer and moved mankind more than any state paper he might have written. In the poem, Milton wrote:

> *"God doth not need*
> *Either man's work or his own gifts. Who best*
> *Bear his mild yoke, they serve him best. His state*
> *Is kingly: thousands at his bidding speed,*
> *And post o'er land and ocean without rest;*
> *They also serve who only stand and wait."*

Handicapped people, speaking among themselves, sometimes refer to others as TAB's, temporarily able-bodied. This is true. All of us will eventually be handicapped, if not by accident or illness, then by old age. Physical limitations are a given in this world. If we peer and listen through instruments beyond our normal human capabilities, we see how severely handicapped even the healthiest of us are. At our prime we cannot hear sound higher than 20,000 cycles per second or lower than about 16 cycles per second. Yet there are audio frequencies extending far beyond our limited listening spectrum. Some other animals do much better than we do in hearing. We cannot see beyond the reds on one end of the color spectrum and the purples on the other. Yet beyond these limitations the ultraviolets stretch out in shorter and shorter wavelengths. The infrareds going the other direction lengthen into heat waves and radio waves. The universe is full of a multitude of sensations that we never know because we are largely deaf and blind. We do not have the sharp eye the eagle has, the speed and quickness of the leopard, the grace of the gazelle, the navigational skills of the migratory birds, the sonar of the bat, the strength of the elephant, or the graceful, undulating swim of the fish. We can jump a little, run rather slowly, and see and hear a few things in this universe.

When we stand in admiration before a beautiful painting, or listen in rapture to great music, or cheer in the stadium for some athletic event, we structure the universe to define our modest human accomplishments as spectacular. We use words such as *genius, maestro,* and *champion* to describe the best of our human efforts. They are superior by human standards, but again, it is human minds that set those standards. Cannot our human minds restructure reality if we are not as mobile as others or have lost the use of some of our sensory perception organs?

Years ago, I stood at the bedside of a beautiful young woman in Idaho. Her thin body had wasted away so that she barely wrinkled the sheet under which she lay. The life had gone out of her limbs, but it seemed to have distilled into her eyes, which sparkled. Using her bright mind, she talked of music she had heard and books she had read. She was up to the minute on the latest happenings in the world. She had not withdrawn into herself. We talked and laughed together. I had gone there to cheer her up, but it was obvious at the end of our talk who had cheered up whom.

For seven years my friend Elwin Pulsipher lay paralyzed with amyotrophic lateral sclerosis (Lou Gehrig's disease). He had been a career army officer, had later earned a doctor's degree in education, and had been an administrator at Brigham Young University. He had been a branch president eleven times, was father to a fine family, a Boy Scout leader, and an active man who loved life. But disease had destroyed virtually all his voluntary muscles and left him dependent on a machine for his every breath. A tube through his throat carried the slurry that was his only nourishment.

Elwin Pulsipher could have seen himself as helpless. Instead he restructured his world with himself as father, patriarch, and leader of his family. He pictured himself as a source of inspiration and strength to others. His tools for helping others were a tiny wisp of a smile and his right eyebrow. No one was ever better at making maximum use of minimum bodily faculties than he. With the smile he could brighten the lives of those who came to visit him. He had his right eyebrow outfitted to actuate a computer. With special writing software he could laboriously compose messages one letter at a time. Write he did. It took him at least twelve hours to write a letter, but he wrote letter after letter to friends, to missionaries in the field, to other handicapped people, encouraging them on. Often he sent me copies of his letters. They always closed with this message, "Have a good day." I felt absolutely obligated to have a good day after an invitation from him. He could have been a captive in his own body. Instead he restructured his world around the abilities he still had.

Stephen Hawking has the same disease as my friend Elwin had and is nearly as paralyzed. Hawking does have the use of three fingers on his right hand and can communicate through a word processor hooked to a voice synthesizer. He can also use his eyes. But his unshackled mind roams among the stars and galaxies, black holes, white holes, and time reversals. He is a world-renowned astrophysicist and author of a best-selling book on the history of time. He is also a man with an unquenchable zest for life. "When one's expectations are reduced to zero, one appreciates everything one does have," he says. He is a mathematics professor at Cambridge University in England, a husband, and father of three. With his powerful mind he has restructured not only his own world, but much of the universe for all of us.

Rosalie Pratt was a concert harpist with a promising career opening before her until a rare disease crippled her fingers. "I was bitter and angry at first," she said. But then she restructured her reality. She saw herself not as a concert performer but as a teacher who could bring special talents and understanding to handicapped students. She has become a world authority in her field. Her gifts in music, her sensitive spirit, and her insight and innovation have brought beauty into lives that were barren. She has helped deaf students to "feel" and "see" music. She developed a special keyboard device that helps them analyze sounds. Through this they can not only learn to appreciate music more, but they can improve their speech rhythm and pitch to make it sound more natural. Rosalie Pratt is not a crippled concert performer. She is a talented, inspiring, and beloved teacher.

A few years ago a talented gymnast from Oregon misjudged

his trampoline jump and landed on his neck. He never used his arms or legs again. Viewed from the outside, his had been an exciting life. As he described it, he had filled his days with wine, women, and revelry. Now the days of satisfying his sensual appetites were over. He was forced inward to his mind and spirit. He surprised everyone, including himself, with the strength and resources he found there. He discovered and developed his mental, emotional, and spiritual abilities. New worlds opened up to him as he sharpened his abilities to perceive them. He restructured his reality to include his new talents and minimize the ones he had lost. Most important, he discovered the Lord and his relationship with Him. The young man often told his story, describing the new life he had developed after his accident. He said of his present condition, "I wouldn't want what happened to me to happen to anyone—unless that's what it takes."

These people and others have shown us how they restructured their reality to minimize their losses and take fullest advantage of the assets they still possessed. The way they and others have successfully restructured their world is a marvel and an inspiration. It shows the tremendous power our minds can have in deciding how we define our losses and what we do about them.

The healing hands of Jesus touched many and made them whole during his short sojourn on the earth. Eventually, his power will heal us all from our handicaps of body, mind, and spirit. Miraculous healings still take place, of course. But perhaps the greatest ongoing miracle is the courage, ingenuity, resourcefulness, and faith shown by those who challenge and overcome physical handicaps. Their victories can be patterns for all of us as we meet the crises that will inevitably come to us in our walk through this world.

Chapter 9

Beautiful Memories Last Forever

Mary Lincoln spent her last days in a darkened room in Springfield, Illinois, where she could live in her memories. She drifted with the days, endlessly caressing her wedding ring with its inscription, "Love Is Eternal." At eventide she would blow out the single candle lighting her room and turn down her side of the bed. She would slip into bed quietly, being careful not to disturb "the President's place" beside her. Some of the neighbors said she was crazy. More accurately, she was probably preserving and nurturing the memories of better times, as all of us do when we suffer a loss.

In undergoing a loss, particularly the loss of a loved one, we may get concerned that the precious experiences we have known before our loss will fade from our memories and be lost also. Sometimes we think of this not just as a personal loss of lovely memories, but as a kind of infidelity to our loved one. We fear that our forgetting may indicate a lack of caring on our part. This concern to preserve the past can cause eccentric and even bizarre behavior. People have been known to let their fondness for memorabilia of the lost one turn into veneration. This is not a healthy mental mode for us. Pictures and souvenirs, of course, are treasured remembrances of the past, but the past is ours to cherish, not to live in.

As for the question of whether we will forget much of our life before our loss, the answer is yes, we will. Our conscious minds are so constructed that we can hold very little in them. Most research indicates that the average person can store about seven digits in his head in short-term memory. We can improve our performance in this area by training and mnemonic devices, but at best our conscious memory can hold only a tiny fraction of what we experience from day to day. Most of us wish we could remember more. Mark Twain described it this way, "The human memory is amazing. It begins working the moment we are born and doesn't stop until we stand up to speak."

A number of factors affect how much we can store in our conscious memory. Age is a factor, though not nearly as big a factor as was once thought. Present research indicates that the elderly who keep their minds active lose only 10 to 15 percent of their memory capacity, unless they're struck with Alzheimer's disease or some other debilitating mental ailment. Emotions play a big part. It's hard to remember things when we are emotionally aroused.

One interesting mental phenomenon is called "flashbulb memory." If you are old enough to remember the day John F. Kennedy was shot or the day Neil Armstrong stepped onto the moon, you can probably remember the circumstances. Unique flashes in your experience tend to stick a long time, although they sometimes get distorted as the years go by. But the conscious short-term memory seems to be quite limited.

In terms of loss, this can be a blessing. If we had our way, we would probably fill our memories with souvenirs, scenes, and memorabilia of the happy times before our loss. Then we would sit in the middle of them and watch the dust settle—watch them turn from souvenirs into antiques, and finally antiquities. We would progress no further. So the Lord in his mercy has made our minds such that the scenes fade quite quickly. They also fade selectively. You have probably noticed that after a short separation from those you love most, even a separation of hours, it's often hard to picture those who are closest to you. Again, there is a reason for that. Abraham Lincoln's son was always frustrated with the photographs of his father. He said they never caught the essence of the man. But then he agreed that it was impossible to capture Abraham Lincoln in a still photograph. His face and his eyes were too animated, constantly changing from twinkling humor to deep sadness. Any picture sliced only a small segment of his total personality.

So it is with our memories of those we love most. We have known their smiles and their sadness; often known them in youth, sometimes in age, in sleep and awake. Our loved one is so varied that when we really know him or her, it's hard for the memory to pick out which image we want when we think back. So we ought not criticize ourselves if the image of those we have loved and lost seems to slip rather quickly from us. That's only an indication of how tightly intertwined our lives are with theirs. Treasured times and beloved companions will fade fairly quickly from our conscious memory. But that is only a temporary phenomenon to allow us to get on with the business of living, which we must be about.

However, there is much more to the story of memory than this. A few years ago in Toronto, Canada, a neurosurgeon by the name of Dr. Wilder Penfield was operating on a patient's brain using local anesthetic. The patient was still conscious even though a section of his skull had been removed, and Dr. Penfield was probing in the gray matter, using a mild electrical current. (This isn't as ghastly as it sounds. The brain has no pain-sensing nerves. The pain of a headache comes from the tissue surrounding the brain.) Dr. Penfield touched an area of the cortex with his probe, which sent a mild electrical signal to the nerves in that area. Suddenly, the patient said, "I see scenes from my childhood." These were not dim recollections. They were startling, full-color scenes complete with sound. In fact, the man began to hum a little song his mother used to sing for him that he hadn't remembered in years. The smells were there, and even the emotions. The entire scene was replayed vividly, literally before the man's eyes. Dr. Penfield probed other areas and aroused other scenes from the man's past.

Dr. Penfield's accidental discoveries opened a whole new area of brain research that is still going on. The more we find out about the mind and the brain, the more we realize we don't know. And we probably never will know the depths of the human mind and soul. One researcher put it this way: if the brain were simple enough for us to understand it, we would be too simple to understand it. Other researchers have duplicated and expanded on Penfield's original probings, but have yet to find really practical applications.

Poking an electrical probe into your skull when a telephone number slips your mind is not a good idea. But in terms of our discussion of loss, Dr. Penfield's discoveries open up marvelous vistas. Such research indicates that absolutely nothing is lost in our journey through this life. Every sight, sound, feeling, touch, thought, and word are still recorded in the billions of neurons in our brains. We are a walking record of everything we have experienced in this life. We may not have access to these limitless records at present, but that is simply because our retrieval system is currently very limited. I believe it is designed so to force us to live in the present where we can control our destinies instead of merely reliving the past over and over again.

But sometime, in the Lord's own appointed hour, I believe all these marvelous memories will be opened to us. I cannot believe they are so carefully and miraculously stored for no reason. Exactly how that is to be done, under what circumstances, and even for what purpose we are not yet told. But we may rest assured that it will come to pass. We needn't concern ourselves, nor condemn ourselves, if our beautiful memories slip quietly into the misty background for a time. They are safely stored, and we will recall them when the time is right.

Chapter 10

Exercise More
Than Your Options

. . . .

A few years ago a newspaper reporter was dying of causes incident to his age and poor physical condition. Understandably, his terminal condition weighed heavily on him mentally and emotionally. He decided to take his own life, and chose an original approach to doing it. He got a set of sweats and running shoes, and one evening set out to run himself to death. He hadn't exercised seriously in years. After a few miles, he fell to the ground exhausted. He dragged himself home to die—but he did not quite die that time, although for a few days he felt like it. He repeated his attempt. Again he felt near death, but survived. He tried again and again. Then a strange thing began to happen. He found he was dying less with every attempt. He even began to get a certain masochistic pleasure from his punishment. He looked forward to it and then to life itself. He not only failed to kill himself with exercise, but he renewed his body and spirit and rejoined the ranks of the healthy and happy in the world.

On any morning I can watch a parade of walkers, joggers, and runners in front of our house. We live on a street with a designated bike path and nice scenery that seems to attract this mobile populace. I have walked or driven that street as early as 4:30 in the morning, and I have yet to be the first person out. Morning and evening, winter and summer, they are there at all hours of the day and most hours of the night. Some of them find an indoor track or shopping mall for the colder weather, but others consider the brisk and even cold weather and change of seasons part of the variety they enjoy in their exercise regimen.

There are no Olympic champions among these walkers and joggers, although a local track club comes up on Wednesday mornings, and they look pretty impressive. Most of them are average people like you and me. And like you and me, they have suffered the various and sundry shocks to body and spirit that come with life. That is one of the reasons they are out there every day. Experts say that a brisk walk, jog, swim, or bicycle ride three times a week is enough to keep most people in acceptable condition. But most of these folks are out every day. There is something more behind their exercise program than sustaining a healthy cardiovascular system. They are using exercise to meet the physical, mental, emotional, and spiritual challenges of each day.

Let me give you a random sample of this passing parade of jogging and walking wounded. Here come Marlin and Barbara Ditmore at a brisk pace. Actually, Marlin is determined to live his whole life at a brisk pace. Approaching his eighth decade with a couple of heart attacks behind him and a bout with pneumonia last winter that left scar tissue on his lungs, Marlin could certainly be excused from the rigors of daily exercise. But he has never looked for excuses in his life and he is not about to start now.

Down the street comes Lyle Koller with a cane. That's great, because a few weeks ago he was pushing a walker. Before then it was a wheelchair, and previous to that he was confined to a hospital and then a home bed when they replaced his hip. Lyle is coming back a step at a time.

Here come Elsbeth Maas and Ruth Naylor. They are animatedly discussing some gospel subject as they cover the miles on their morning constitutional. Part of their discussion probably centers on the afterlife, because there used to be three of those lovely sisters. These two had helped the third one clear her lungs of asthma. Later their friend died slowly of cancer. They encouraged and cheered her on as long as she was able to walk with them.

Down the street comes another good neighbor from a few

blocks away. Her husband's business is not doing well. They may lose it and perhaps their home as well. This daily walk relaxes her and helps to clear her mind and give her strength to face their present and future problems.

My friend Dave's wife left a few years ago. Nobody knows why. They seemed happy enough. Dave gets out most mornings to greet his friends and neighbors and work his way back from the lonely nights. Daily exercise is the common bond of these and tens of thousands more who are using this powerful weapon of defense against depression, anxiety, and discouragement.

Physical exercise may be one of the last resources we think of in a time of discouragement, but it can help us to increase our motivation as we try to pick up the pieces and go on after a loss. Research is showing the mind and the body to be more tightly locked together than we ever suspected. They cause each other to get up and get down.

People sometimes ask me how to get going on a physical fitness program. Here is how: slowly. S-l-o-w-l-y. It is almost impossible to start too slowly. Usually we want fast results, so we leap in with more gusto than wisdom. Our unaccustomed muscles naturally complain, and by about the third day we decide the gain isn't worth the pain and we give it up. My suggestion for the first day out is to pull on your gym shoes and tighten them up, then loosen them and take them off. That will do it for the first day. Hit the showers. Leave yourself wanting more. All right, this is exaggerated a little, but not much. Take it slowly, particularly in a down time such as a loss brings on.

A second word of advice is to find activities that you enjoy. Most people like to walk or jog. But some prefer swimming or cycling. For mental relaxation and refreshment you are generally better off choosing gentle, noncompetitive exercises, but choose the ones that come fairly naturally to you and bring you a sense of satisfaction when you do them. My experience is that if you choose these kinds of activities and start slowly, you will find physical exercise very helpful in coming back from the mental and emotional despondency loss can bring on.

Running may not be your preferred form of workout, and that's fine. The heart doesn't know the difference between running, walking rapidly, bicycling, swimming, and other exercises that use the big muscles in a regular and rhythmic fashion. Basically, what you are trying to do is use the large muscles, particularly the muscles in your legs, to force-feed your heart. These muscles contract rhythmically as you exercise. In doing so, they squeeze the big veins inside of them and send blood under pressure back to the heart. Then every time the heart valve opens to take a sip of blood, it meets this pressurized stream the muscles are sending to it. The chamber is forced to stretch a little to accommodate more of the blood than it had planned to. Over thousands of such stretchings, the heart's capacity grows. It is able to pump more blood with every beat. This accomplishes two purposes. First, the heart can do an equal amount of work with fewer beats. This allows it to work less to keep you going.

Second, and perhaps more important in a discussion of pulling up out of depression, the heart pumps more blood with every stroke. This blood is rich in oxygen because exercise also develops the lungs' capacity to hold more air and extract oxygen from it more efficiently. Oxygen is the breakfast, lunch, and dinner of champions. When we are low on oxygen, we feel sluggish. Our muscles have no energy, our brain is blurred, and our mind sees the grim side of every situation. These are all physiological states, but I can't think of a better description of emotional depression than this. There are usually other factors, but a mere shortage of oxygen in our system can depress us singlehandedly.

On the other hand, a healthy heart pumping strong streams of oxygen-enriched blood can be a powerful warrior in our battle against the blues. This is not the only reason that aerobic exercise can strengthen us against depression. Sir Isaac Newton's laws of motion apply to human beings as well. He said, "A body in motion tends to remain in motion, unless acted upon by an opposing force." The actual and symbolic process of putting one foot in front of the other one reminds us that we are not dead. We are live bodies in motion; and if nothing else, there is always the chance we may stumble upon an answer to our problems.

Good counsel to people who are flattened by depression is to try to get the monkey off their back by getting the mattress off their back. I'm not saying it's easy, and chemical imbalances and other personal problems may add to the weight of the burden they are carrying. But the counsel is still very good. When you are moving, you are generally a proactive and not a reactive force. You are constantly changing the environment around you – even a little, even from one room to another. You are meeting new situations and new people. Each of these has the potential of containing a shaft of light that may help to lead you from the darkness.

The body itself was made for movement. When it is fulfilling the measure of its creation, even in awkward stumbles or creaky-jointed crawling, it rewards us. When we are active, the brain releases endorphins. These are natural tranquilizers that help to raise our spirits and calm our anxieties. They can even help counteract chemical imbalances that may be causing our depression. Exercise tends to make us feel and look younger, and this can help brighten our spirits. It can give us the feeling that we are in control of our bodies. Then we can extend that control outward from our being to our immediate surroundings and environment. We may surprise ourselves at how far-reaching the effects of even a modest exercise program can be.

Chapter 11

Don't Fight on Two Fronts

Adolph Hitler was an evil man but a military and political master strategist, according to historian William L. Shirer. But he made one fatal miscalculation. He tried simultaneously to defeat Russia on the east and the Allies on the west. In so doing, he added the mighty Third Reich war machine to the junk pile of military history. He joined the company of commanders who have tried to fight on two fronts at the same time. It almost never works.

This principle is wise generalship when we face the battle to overcome a loss in our lives. The struggle can draw heavily on our resources. Like a general, we must commit our fighting forces of every sort. Our physical strength, our mental abilities, our emotional power, and our spiritual reserves may be called on as they have never been before.

If our minds are distracted and our mental powers dissipated, we have less strength to fight the battle of the mind that wages whenever we suffer a loss. Worry is a natural temptation at these times. We often worry about what the future now holds for us. Will we be able to pay the bills and meet the demands of each day? What if this is only the beginning of a series of losses? If it is a business loss, what will this do to our financial position and our standing among our peers and in the community? If it is a loss of reputation or of face, due to some mistake we have made, our mind flits from face to face of our acquaintances, worrying about what they will think. If we have lost a loved one, particularly in an accident, we are tempted to think, "Could I have done something differently to avoid this?" All manner of devious paths are open to our minds, and they love to keep us busy following them. But they run away with our mental strength if we let them.

How, then, do we keep a tight rein on our minds? We don't. What we really need to do with our minds is not try to pull them back. Our minds are marvelous, frisky, wide-ranging, inquisitive creatures. Like spirited hunting dogs, they are always out in front of us sniffing the air, poking under bushes, exploring the nooks and crannies of our environment for new information. They don't respond well to negative commands and tight leashes. If we tell them to stop and stay, they come back momentarily, but then they whine and complain and are soon bounding off again in the wrong direction. Rather than reining and muzzling them, we need to make use of their incorrigible curiosity. We should set out a goal in front of our minds, then instruct them to get us to that goal. When we find our minds wandering into forbidden or un-fruitful paths, rather than castigating them and calling them home, we need merely to remind them where the goal is. They will pick up the trail from where they are and refocus on the target. They will do even better than this: very often our wandering minds will use the information they've gathered, even in side trips, to help guide them on toward the goal.

So as we map out our campaign strategy to win the battle over loss, the first thing we must do is what every general does. We must point at the battle map and say, "We are here, and we want to get to there." We need to tell our minds what goal we are trying to reach. What does it look like? What is the terrain, the environment, the population? War strategists often talk about getting the big picture. The foot soldier in the trenches may not know any more than his job to take the next hill in the next battle, but somebody in the army had better have a vision of the big picture, or the campaign is lost before it begins. The metaphor is appropriate in our mental battles. We need to get the big picture of our goal. What will it look like when we have overcome our loss? What will the landscape be like? What personnel—whom will we be with? What will we be like? Will we have gained additional attributes and character strengths through the struggle?

All this information, like reconnaissance to a general, must be constantly fed into our minds to flesh out the image of the goal we are striving to achieve. Then this image must be constantly transmitted to the fighting mental forces under our control. Whenever our minds wander off to worries or fears, we should give them the picture of the goal to pull them around and send them off on the right course again. The mind is perhaps our most powerful resource. This is our heavy artillery in the battle to overcome loss. No wonder we often lose battles, when we turn our guns upon ourselves.

The emotions are so closely tied to the mind and they overlap in so many ways that it is impossible to say where one stops and the other begins. For that matter, it is impossible to say where the physical person—or the mental, or the emotional, or the spiritual—stops. They overlap on every edge. They are like strings on a harp, and you cannot pluck one without having the tone resound and reverberate throughout the entire system. A physical ailment focuses our minds upon it. This affects our emotions negatively, and can even impinge on our spiritual well-being. Likewise, emotional lows can bring on pessimistic thoughts and psychosomatic physical illnesses, and scar over our spiritual sensitivity. Spiritual and emotional traumas have stupefied the minds and blighted the health of many people. Richard Nixon developed phlebitis shortly after he was forced to resign. Lyndon Johnson was not the same robust cowboy after his public policies were largely rejected and he was denied the opportunity to run for president a second time. Medical research indicates that the will to live can be a powerful factor in whether people survive serious illnesses.

The practical point of all this observation and speculation is that we can wage war against defeat on the battlefield of our emotions as we can in the other areas of our lives. We are not helpless hostages to external events. But again, we probably do not have the strength to fight on two fronts. We must make a good, substantial peace within ourselves so that we can conserve our emotional strength to fight the external opposition.

Charlie Plumb learned this lesson early in his captivity in North Vietnam. His external opposition was almost overwhelming. Locked in a bamboo dungeon in solitary confinement, baking in the soggy jungle heat, retching on rotten food, covered with sores and boils, existing in putrid squalor, cut off from virtually all sources of outward strength (not even a window to peer out of), he should have died. He almost did. But one day a more experienced prisoner smuggled a note to him that saved his life. The note explained a system through which they could communicate by jiggling a wire back and forth between their two isolated cells. Gradually, Charlie learned to translate the jiggles on the wire into words, and he began to communicate with his friend. Charlie poured out his anger and self-pity at having been plucked by fate from the skies as a high-flying Navy pilot five days before he was scheduled to be rotated back home. In an instant he had lost everything and dropped from being top gun and king of the clouds to a wretched, muddy rat in a rice paddy. He was understandably bitter.

His experienced fellow prisoner told him he was perfectly free to have those feelings, and was probably justified. He said, "Go ahead and feel that way if you want to, Charlie, but there is one thing you should know: it will cost you your life." He then recounted to Charlie the stories of other prisoners who had devoured themselves in self-pity and died.

In that instant, Charlie made the choice to be a survivor. He stopped wasting his emotional ammunition on himself and saved it for the enemy outside — not only his North Vietnamese captors, but the silent enemies of loneliness, fear, isolation, nostalgia, and heartbreak. He settled within himself the question of why he was there. He decided that for some good reason God had put him there, or allowed him to be there. That was all he knew and all he needed to know. Then he got on to the really important question of what to do about it. He said, among other things, "Do you know how many church hymns you can dredge up out of your memory if you have seven years to think about it? In my case the answer is seventy-eight." He remembered and repeated snatches of the Bible he had been taught in church, other literature, training instructions, and information from his school days. Most important for his emotional battle, he kept his self-conversations upbeat. He sought out and found joy in even the tiniest blessings of life. He could literally, as the scriptures say, give thanks for his latest breath. By fighting on only one front, Charlie Plumb won the battle against what would seem to be overwhelming odds, and he survived. The same principles can apply to us in overcoming our own losses, big and small.

Every night we ask each of our children a couple of questions. One of them is, "What was your happiest thing today?" Like most children, indeed almost all of us, they sometimes have a hard time thinking of anything happy. "Nothing good happened today," they have sometimes said.

Then we ask them some other questions: "Did you get out of bed this morning?"

"Yes."

"A lot of people didn't. Did you have breakfast?"

"Yes."

"A lot of people didn't—a lot of people went hungry all day and went to bed hungry tonight. And they will do the same thing every day for the rest of their lives."

It doesn't take long to find a happiest thing. We hope that a lifetime of this daily emotional exercise will help them to pick out automatically the good things in every day's activities. Then they can be at peace within themselves and have more strength to win the battles against outward opposition.

In the physical aspects of our existence, we also tend to divide our forces and try to battle on two fronts at once. In our exterior world the laws of gravity and inertia are ever present and ever powerful. They want to pull us down and stop our progress. If we have been weakened by loss or grief, we have disrupted the balance between the forces we have used to keep us active and the ever-present resistance that would slow us down or stop us. It is harder to get going in the morning; harder to keep a daily work schedule; harder to do aerobic exercises that would help pump new oxygen, life, and energy into our bodies. It is harder to smile, look up, and speak cheerfully.

In a state of depression, it is easy to look at our face and form and feel old, used up, wrinkled and wasted, or flabby and overweight. But when we cave in to these feelings and treat our bodies and our physical surroundings accordingly, we turn them into enemies. On the other hand, the more we discipline our bodies, the more we can control them and thereby control the outward environment around us. To be sure, our physiques are subject to the slings and arrows of outrageous fortune. They will inevitably get creaky and cranky and take more skill and inner strength to operate. But that will be a source of depression to us only if we make it so. We can choose to consider it a quiet challenge that can bring us increased mental, emotional, and spiritual power.

George Lucas, the creator of the "Star Wars" series of motion pictures, is one of the most successful directors in the business. He understands the principle that getting the most out of an old body can sometimes be more intriguing than zipping around in a new one. In the first "Star Wars" episode, his heroes whipped through space in their rocket ship, the Millennium Falcon. In a sci-fi flick such as this, you would expect the main characters' transportation to be shiny and studded with high-tech bells and whistles. But Lucas is too clever a writer and director to pass up this golden opportunity to pluck the heartstrings of his viewers. The Millennium Falcon is an antiquated, interstellar hot rod—a tin can that is always technologically behind the sophisticated spaceships of the evil empire. Only the skill and ingenuity of her owner/pilot/mechanic, Han Solo, keep her aloft and out of the clutches of the enemy. He knows where and when to bang around with his space-age monkey wrench every time she coughs or sputters or gets off course.

This aesthetic element of the human mind and spirit overcoming the limitations of the physical world adds tremendously to our interest and empathy with the protagonists in the movie.

The same is true in our real lives. There is great satisfaction and growth in working out our destinies through physical imperfections and with bodies that gradually grow older and less efficient.

Some who do not understand have criticized the leaders of the Church as being too old and infirm to function in their heavy responsibilities. These people miss the point entirely. It is precisely because of their age, and sometimes physical impairment, that they develop the powerful mental and spiritual muscles they need to lead the kingdom. Spencer W. Kimball was a man small of stature, dogged with serious ailments all the years of his later life, robbed by cancer of most of his voice, precariously balancing his medications to keep his blood thin enough to course through his aged arteries but thick enough not to rupture again in the capillaries of his brain. Working around and through this unstable physical situation, he added to his spiritual strength. He was a giant in the land, a man whose strength and vision we have scarcely begun to comprehend, much less fulfill.

The physical battle can likewise build us if we fight it on a single front. But if we see our weakening bodies as a sign of weakening will, we may turn our bodies into "fifth columnists." You may recall the story of an ancient general attacking a fortified city. He had planted subversives and insurrectionists inside the city, ready to cripple its defenses when the attack began. An observer commented on his armies, which were marching in four columns against the outward walls. The general said, "Yes, I have four columns, but inside I have a fifth column that may be more effective than any of the others." Hence the term "fifth columnists" for those who sabotage the war effort from the inside.

The spiritual battleground is the most important aspect of our lives. We may survive the loss of physical health, friends and social standing, mental abilities and competence. But if we lose the battle of the spirit, our loss can have eternally tragic consequences. It is in the realms of the spirit that we need to marshal our resources, focus them on the opposition, and, as the Apostle Paul said, "Fight the good fight." (1 Timothy 6:12.) The enemies of the spirit are deeply entrenched in our outside environment.

The lust for power, material possessions, sensual gratification, ease and indolence, selfishness and greed, and other vices are constantly blazing away at our spiritual selves. From the heavy artillery of lust and avarice to the small-arms fire of gossip and criticism, they lay out a constant barrage against our spiritual defenses. If we are to survive this continual onslaught from the outside, surely we need to keep ourselves entrenched in solid spiritual fortifications.

A loss in our lives can create a breach in the wall. We may turn bitter and curse God and our own creation for putting us in a situation where tragedy could occur to us. We may even blame God as the cause of our trials. If we do not face our losses with spiritual strength, the enemy will pour through our defenses and overrun our city. And as with any military maneuver, he will be much harder to drive out once he is in than to keep out while he is still at bay.

We fortify our spiritual defenses through reading and pondering the scriptures, through praying and fasting, and through serving others—particularly in building up the Lord's kingdom. These activities strengthen us against the adversary. Scripture study and contemplation help to give us an eternal perspective of our temporary loss. Fasting builds our spiritual muscles and gives us greater control over our bodies. It can even help us control the chemical and hormonal imbalances that can exacerbate our depressions during times of loss. Prayer opens the conduit to heaven and allows the Holy Ghost, the Comforter, to speak peace to our souls. Service to others keeps us moving, gets our minds off ourselves, and helps speed the passage of time. If we are in the proper frame of mind and spirit, time is the most powerful healing balm with which to soothe the wounds of loss and grief.

There will be wounds in these battles. We can, and should, fortify our physical, mental, emotional, and spiritual defenses, but we can never make them impregnable. We can skillfully align our fighting forces; we can minimize the battlefronts on which we must simultaneously fight. All these are solid and responsible military tactics, but there is one more factor that must be present if we are to achieve the victory.

General Ulysses S. Grant is not remembered as a military tactical genius. He was competent, but not breathtaking in strategy. But the *U.S.* in Grant's name stood for something more than Ulysses Simpson. It stood for "unconditional surrender" when he went into battle. This tenacious bulldog would "fight it out on this line if it takes all summer." If necessary, he would fight a protracted war of attrition until his forces wore down the opposition.

In a sense, every war is a war of attrition. Superb generalship and a few victories in battle count for little if we do not have the strength to persevere until the war is won. In our personal battles, this is called "enduring to the end." Then, after that ultimate victory, we shall eventually enjoy eternal peace.

Traveling Tips

· ·

Here are some suggestions to help you move through this part of your journey in overcoming your loss:

Find ways to put additional information into your mind. Use a variety of activities: reading, viewing uplifting motion pictures and videos, listening to records, attending live concerts and plays, browsing in museums, talking with other people, traveling, building things, growing plants, caring for animals. All these are good. The subject matter is not as important as the tone of the activities. Try to put in upbeat, optimistic raw material for your mind to work on. Your mind and heart may react cynically at first and suspect you of trying to lead them away from their dedicated purpose of grief and mourning. That's exactly what you are doing, and after a while the additional information will lodge in your mind and heart and begin to take effect.

Reach out to help others. This is strong medicine when you yourself are in such need of help. Like other strong medicine, it is hard to take, but it is very powerful — perhaps the most powerful medicine of all next to prayer. Look about you at others who may be suffering loss. Are there ways you could help them get through their crises? Plan to do so.

Read and discuss the lives of others with particular attention to the part that loss has played in their progress. Antonio Stra-

divari, who was disappointed at not being a great violinist, instead began building violins and became the greatest at his craft. Abraham Lincoln lost election after election but in the process developed his values, his style, and his empathy, becoming one of the greatest presidents in U.S. history. Winston Churchill failed in his plans in World War I but used the experience to prepare himself to lead Britain in World War II. Lehi lost his fine business in Jerusalem, Peter his fishing operation. Both gained immortality and eternal life by accepting those losses.

Look at your own history and note where losses and disappointments have changed the direction of your life. What benefits may have accrued to you because of your losses?

As much as possible, avoid far-reaching, life-changing decisions for a while. Your judgment is still heavily affected by your loss. In an effort to fill the void in your life or avoid constant reminders of your loss, you may want to make sweeping changes in your career or your personal life. Listen to the counsel of those whose judgment you trust and who are near enough to you to be deeply sensitive to your needs, but far enough away from the loss that their counsel is not as emotionally affected as yours may be.

On the other hand, feel free to make changes when the time is right. The right time will usually be some months after a serious loss, but not always. It may come sooner or later with different individuals. The right time is when the initial pain and shock have almost worn off. It is when the routine has settled in and given you a chance to evaluate the good and the not-so-good aspects of your present situation. The right time is when you have studied the alternatives of the decision you are considering and taken counsel from trusted associates and authorities. But ultimately, the right time is after you have pondered and prayed, set your life in order as well as you know how, and asked for the Holy Spirit of the Lord to guide your actions. He will. Then feel free to move.

Refurbish and visit often your mental place of relaxation and refuge. This place, you will remember, is the mental utopia you created not long after your loss. It is the place in which all your dreams are fulfilled and things are as perfect as your imagination can conceive them. Visualize this scene. What are the sights, the sounds, the smells, the feelings? It's fine and natural if this scene includes conditions before your loss. That won't hurt. Feel free to put the scene anywhere you want and populate it with whatever people you choose or with just yourself. Picture your scene in great detail. Is it day or night? Is it winter, spring, summer, or fall? Is it indoors or outdoors? Who is there with you? In whatever ways you can, make the scene more vivid and pleasant for yourself. It is perfectly all right to include people and situations that were near you before your loss, because you are not merely reliving the past. You are creating a pleasant place for your mind to dwell during its future hard times—drawing up blueprints for a future condition that will eventually exist. This is far different from neurotically bogging down in the time before your loss and staying there.

Picture yourself drawing power and strength to your body and spirit. Loss can be weakening, even debilitating, if we let it. The long, gray grind can wear you down. You need sources of mental and physical strength. It is important that you care for your body with proper food and rest, exercise and good health habits. Let your mind assist in this power-producing process. As you eat good food, picture it being absorbed into your system and spreading strength and good health throughout your body. As you breathe, think of the energy-producing oxygen in the air. Feel this power tingle right down to your fingertips and toes. Think of each breath drawn as added strength gained.

Finally, be patient. Every tick of the clock and turning of the world is a victory for you as you work through the long, gray grind.

Part 3

Overcoming,
Not Just Enduring

Milestone Markers

This is the third stage of your journey in overcoming your loss. In this stage you will go beyond enduring the loss and seek to overcome it. As in the other stages you have come through, this part of the terrain is uphill, but it can be mastered. This is a vital segment of your journey. It is the process by which you turn your loss from a stumbling block to a stepping stone on your way to godhood. You can take strength and encouragement from the progress you have already made.

The road ahead is marked by levels that, when achieved, will in fact extract blessings from your loss — blessings for you and for those fortunate enough to be touched by your influence.

As with the previous milestones, you will probably not yet have arrived at these. But as you continue your journey, you will one day be able to say these things to yourself:

I am more responsible for my own life, having overcome this loss. I do not blame my difficulties on my environment or on other people. I take responsibility for my actions.

I have a firmer faith and trust in God.

I believe God will send me nothing that is not for my ultimate good.

I am more committed to developing my character and effectiveness as a valuable human being.

I am less committed to accumulating worldly possessions as a goal for my life.

I am less committed to obtaining glory, praise, or power as a goal for my life.

I am more sensitive to the sufferings of others and I am involved in helping to alleviate those sufferings because of what I have gone through.

If my loss could have been prevented by my actions, I have developed strategies to help prevent such a loss from happening again.

I can see clearly ways in which this loss has been beneficial to me, and I am grateful for those aspects of my loss.

I do not fear the future even though it may contain losses similar to the one I have suffered in the past. I see loss as another gift from a loving God to help me and my fellow human beings progress and grow.

I am actively involved in the lives of others and seek ways to help them.

I am not a victim of the world's circumstances. I am a stronger and more confident person and less intimidated by the possibility of loss in my life.

I am not a casual observer in the world's suffering; I am a force for good.

I have a greater depth and breadth of understanding of this life and the important things in it. I more often measure my activities and the events of my life in an eternal perspective.

I am a wiser and more efficient person because of my understanding of the place of loss in my life and the lives of others.

Chapter 12

Not Just Enduring,
but Overcoming

· ·

When it comes to loss, we might divide people into three categories: those who suffer loss, those who endure loss, and those who overcome loss. The first category includes every person who ever drew breath. No human being ever took the journey from cradle to grave without some painful steps along the way and some unpleasant wandering in wildernesses.

The second category includes most people. A few sad folks get totally crushed by their losses and never recover, but most people struggle back, battered and scarred. They try to pick up the pieces as best they can and go on living.

But a few interpret their loss as opportunity. I knew a man who had one standard line whenever things went wrong, which they often did in his life. He would say, "Boy, I can't believe what kind of person I'll be when I get through this." And he was right. Like fine-tempered steel, it seemed the more he got hammered on the stronger he became. This marvelous metamorphosis doesn't take place automatically, of course. It takes commitment, fortitude, and powerful internal visualization to bring it about.

Survivors have certain traits in common, according to researchers. They bend instead of break. They have a solid sense of their self-worth. They often act intuitively, and those decisions turn out well for them. They have a strong outward focus in their lives, looking for the needs of others more than concentrating on their own problems. They are able to change directions with relatively little trauma, and they have a generally optimistic outlook.

Overcomers start with these same traits and then build upon them. I talked with one woman who was putting her life together after twenty-one years of physical and psychological abuse in a relationship misnamed "marriage." She finally sought for and obtained a divorce and endured the trauma that always accompanies that terrible experience. It was the struggle of her life to overcome two decades of having her gentle feelings and her personal worth drained by an insensitive man who tried to make her believe she was worthless. The very real grief of the divorce for her and their children added to her burden. But little by little she was making her way back. Her combined losses had forced her into a situation where she either had to give up and live on other people's handouts and pity or dig deep and come up with strength and resources she had never had before. She chose to dig in instead of give up. She gathered her courage and applied for a good job as a court clerk. She moved to another town and started a new life.

This woman said, "I was terribly unhappy in our marriage. I didn't want to leave, but there seemed to be no other way. And now life goes on. I can either be bitter and negative or try to make the best for me, my children, and my former husband out of the situation that I have now." She is presently enduring quite successfully and beginning the process of overcoming, I believe.

To turn a corner from enduring into overcoming requires that we believe in change and growth. It requires that we be builders and not breakers. Substantial builders need a solid foundation of optimism. This does not mean we have to go around giggling all the time. Optimists have their down times like everyone else. The young woman I just told you about said, "When I am in those hard situations, I'm often sad and bitter. But if I can get away from the pain for a while, I can get my head together and see that this isn't the end of the world. I can come back."

Being optimistic does not require changing our basic character so much as remembering what we used to be. Virtually every human being is born an optimist. Every infant believes that if it cries, help will come — if it reaches out, someone will take its hand. Every toddler believes that somewhere beyond the bumped noses and skinned knees lies the golden land of walking. Every kid daydreams heroic stories with himself or herself in the starring role. Even rebellious teenagers behave as they do because they feel they are big enough and smart enough now that the world should take them more seriously. At heart we all believe, or used to believe, that we are important. For most of us there is no sweeter sound on earth than our own name. A sincere compliment from someone we admire can warm us to the core. Inside we know we are good and valuable people. To change this optimism requires that we allow the world to beat it out of us. Outward circumstances provide the refining fire, but it is our decision whether the fire melts us down or purifies and tempers us.

A few years ago a young Cambodian girl escaped with her family into the jungles of Southeast Asia. All the other family members were killed or captured. She faced death many times, but finally made her way to the coast. She worked there for months until an opportunity came to risk her life on a leaky, unseaworthy boat. She took the chance, beat the odds, and made it to America. Alone in a strange land with a foreign culture and an unknown tongue, she continued her fight for survival. She studied relent- lessly, eventually graduated from high school and college, and was later named the "Teacher of the Year" in America. Nothing in her outward environment encouraged her to believe that she could accomplish that incredible odyssey, but inside she was listening to the voice of a child who believed that she could make it and that life was worth the struggle.

This is the basic decision that we all have to make. Is this life, in its temporal and its eternal definitions, worth the struggle? If we say yes, we are basically optimists, and eventually we will overcome all the trials that may be heaped on us. If we allow ourselves to give up the basic optimism we were born with, we have turned to pessimism, and we will not have the strength to win life's battles. Eventually, even a straw can flatten us. We may perish just from boredom if we let defeat become our basic mode of thought. But that is a choice we consciously make.

We are born with an upward reach, a homesickness for heaven from whence we came and to which we shall return if we are willing. The upward path to overcoming our loss requires effort, but it is, in the long run, less difficult than the downward journey of caving in and giving up. Because the efforts we make climbing are productive efforts, they are rewarding. They allow us to look back with satisfaction over the terrain we have covered and take renewed strength for the climb ahead. We can see that we are a little stronger and more able to continue for having come this far on the journey. This is one application of Christ's teaching, "My yoke is easy, and my burden is light." (Matthew 11:30.) The road is not a downhill coast but an inspiring and fulfilling uphill climb. We are promised that whenever our steps falter, the Savior and his Holy Spirit will be there to lift us up and strengthen our feeble knees along the path. We have no such promise when we are going the other direction. There is no stagnant, holding, neutral position in our eternal journey. We are always going one direction or the other. We are overcoming or being overcome by the challenges and the losses of life.

It matters not how far we have come on the journey or where we are on the ladder. What is important is which direction our face is pointed. If we are on the top rung looking down, we are in more jeopardy than the person on the bottom rung looking up. It matters not what losses we have overcome before. The deciding factor for our present state is how we are handling the loss that lies presently before us. From scripture and from our own experience, we know that God will not drown us in a sea of circumstances beyond our control. But neither will he insult us by giving us knee-deep water after we have learned to be skillful swimmers. The challenges in this second estate will be gauged and measured and custom-fitted to our capacities to handle them. We'll face nothing that we cannot overcome with the Lord's help.

Our losses will come in three categories. The first type of loss we suffer simply by coming into a world that is imperfect, temporary, and subject to unexplainable problems and even tragedies. The second category consists of losses we bring upon ourselves through carelessness and sin. The third category is losses the Lord deliberately sends to teach us and strengthen us and to develop our character. All these losses are difficult, but none are insurmountable. We can conquer the losses that are merely a part of this imperfect world if we understand that this second estate is only temporary, and that eventually even the unexplained injustices will be corrected. The losses we bring upon ourselves through sin are, thank heaven, subject to the atoning power of the Savior. Although we may have brought suffering and pain upon ourselves and upon others, if we have faith in Christ, throw ourselves upon his mercy, and do all that we can to repent and make recompense for our sins, we can eventually overcome these tragic losses also. The losses the Lord sends upon us to help us along our individual paths to perfection are, in the measurement of a longer perspective, not losses at all, but testing and training exercises for us. In those cases our best response is to try to understand the will of the Lord, match our limited vision to his eternal perspective, and meet the challenge in accordance with his divine will.

Whatever the challenge, the apparent setback, or the heartbreaking loss, we need to meet it, endure it, and overcome it. If we do not, it will be forever an obstacle in the path of our continued progress and eventual godhood. This may seem like a difficult doctrine when we are lying limp and bleeding from a loss in our lives. But in actuality it is the most encouraging philosophy we could have to live by. It tells us that eventually, with God's help, we can overcome every trial and someday arrive at the point where personal loss is only a past memory. At that day we will receive the blessed reward from our God for being faithful in the face of adversity. We can inscribe our own names on the testimony of the Apostle Paul, "I have fought a good fight, I have finished my course, I have kept the faith: Henceforth there is laid up for me a crown of righteousness, which the Lord, the righteous judge, shall give me at that day: and not to me only, but unto all them also that love his appearing." (2 Timothy 4:7–8.)

Chapter 13

You've Paid the Price,
Now Take the Prize

· ·

" 'Give,' said the little stream, 'Give, oh give, give, oh give . . . '
singing, singing all the day, 'Give, oh give away.' " The lilting
little melody and the simple but profound lyrics floated out of the
big playback speakers and across the recording studio at Capitol
Records in Hollywood, California. The engineer smiled and the
record producer smiled. Dick Davis, Denis Sorenson, and I (The
Three D's), who had just recorded the song, all smiled. It was a
beautiful little record with "hit" stamped all over it. The timing
was perfect; it was the early 1960s. The popular-music public was
temporarily tired of "moon, June, croon, spoon" lyrics and was
looking for music with a little more message. The acid rockers
had not yet erupted on the scene with their antiestablishment
musical propaganda, which would soon drown out everything else
for a few years. Folk music with a message, and sometimes a
moral, was enjoying a brief season or two of popularity. It was a
time of hootenannies and sing-alongs, of the Kingston Trio, the
Limelighters, the Brothers Four, the New Christy Minstrels, the
Smothers Brothers, and a few hundred other pickers and singers
and joke tellers.

Not long before, a Catholic nun had made a hit record with
a song titled "Dominique." The timing was perfect for "Give,
Said the Little Stream." And obviously, the Three D's were the
perfect group to sing it. Dick, Denis, and I had grown up through
Primary singing this little song. We were all returned missionaries

and dedicated to continuing to spread the gospel with our talents. Dick and Denis were married, and I soon would be. We needed the money. If ever a hit record were written in the stars, it was this one. Capitol Records thought so, too. They enthusiastically pressed the record, sent it to the radio stations, and sat poised at their cash registers waiting for the results.

There was just one problem, we found out later. For the first time in the history of that venerable record company, they punched the hole in the record off center. The radio station program directors and DJs across the country dropped it on the turntables; heard about sixteen bars of wobbling, wailing music; and decided the public wasn't ready for this new sound. They dropped it immediately into the trash can. You can believe that story or not, but that's what the record company told us. Whatever the reasons, "Give, Said the Little Stream" went bravely singing, singing all the day into the wilderness of the record marketplace and never returned. It sold a few copies over the years, but it never became the great hit record it might have been. And the Three D's never rode that record to international stardom. It was a golden opportunity lost.

Now we had to decide what to do about it. We could blame the record company, mourn our misfortune, and quit. We chose not to. We did our share of blaming and moaning, but we didn't quit. Instead we went back to the rehearsal hall and the recording studio and off on the college coffeehouse circuit, to develop a satisfying career that lasted for the next sixteen years. We never got the blazing spotlights and the big money that come with stardom, but we got things that, in the long run, may have been better for us professionally and in our service to the Lord's kingdom.

I noticed that those who got success early were locked into a certain image, music style, and even particular songs. One night I listened to Peter, Paul and Mary sing "Puff, the Magic Dragon" for the umpteen thousandth time. They admitted they were very tired of singing the song, but the audience demanded it. Stars were often prisoners of their own popularity. They didn't dare—nor would their audience allow them—to grow, change, and continue to develop and display new talents.

We, on the other hand, were forced to develop new material constantly. We played audiences that varied from elementary school to the elderly—from the Rose Bowl to the rice paddies of Vietnam. At one time we had eight solid hours of varied material from which we drew music and comedy adapted to almost every conceivable audience. It was hard work over the years, but I believe we grew and developed more than we would have done had we spent those sixteen years singing "Give, Said the Little Stream" and other recorded hits. Now, please don't ask me to make a choice. I'm not saying I would not have enjoyed having "Give, Said the Little Stream" and other songs of ours sweep the record charts. I'm just saying that when we lost that opportunity, there was a trade-off. And there always is, in every loss in our lives.

Abraham voluntarily lost the most fertile parts of the promised land. He gave them to his nephew, Lot. As it turned out, Abraham got in trade a lifetime of struggle and disappointment that culminated in his being the "father of the faithful." Lot got the fertile fields, the easy life, and the bright lights of the big cities in Sodom and Gomorrah.

In many transactions we take a loss. Every time we purchase a product we give money, goods, or services in return. If we receive what we consider to be sufficient value in exchange for what we pay, we do not consider that a loss. In a good investment we get back more than we give and are more than satisfied with having sacrificed something in exchange. But if we get little or nothing back for our money, we feel shortchanged and cheated, and rightly so.

Perhaps Americans, above all people, have internalized this spirit of the Yankee trader as a natural way of living life. I have done some work in advertising and know that the average American homemaker, for example, is a pretty hard sell. The men, from my experience, don't appear to be as articulate about what they will and will not buy and pay for, but they are equally effective. They just quietly walk away and don't come back. This mentality is not limited to one section of the country or one social, vocational, or economic stratum among us. The simple, country farmer outfoxing the city slicker is standard fare in our folklore. The fast-talking car salesman, the high-powered lawyer, and the pork-barreling politician all have two things in common: they are looking for a good deal for themselves, and they are all as American as apple pie. There are some drawbacks to these national characteristics, but there are advantages, too. One is that we tend to demand good measure for our money, a fair return for our effort, a fair day's work for a fair day's pay, and goods and services worth the price we give for them. The system doesn't work perfectly, but it has helped to make our standard of living the envy of much of the world.

I suggest we take that same mental set into our consideration of loss in our lives. Frequently, we don't. We tend to write off loss as a good thing gone forever. We uncharacteristically sit and sigh over what we have been called upon to give, without a thought of what we might get in return. I believe we shortchange ourselves when we passively accept loss with no payment in return. We ought to stand up and demand our rightful dues. If we do so, I believe that the world, the universe, our own psychological and emotional makeup, and the Lord himself will respect those rights.

Nothing irritates me more than to have my car or truck break down. To take them to a garage, pay out my good money, and bring them home only as good as they were before somehow seems like wasting money to me. If I possibly can, I have the mechanics do something else while they are there, even though it costs a little more—replace a fan belt, fix a muffler or a rattle that has been bothering me, along with the major problem—anything so that I get something additional for my money.

I suggest we take this sort of hardheaded business approach to loss. We pay a great deal in grief, bereavement, money, ulcers, lost sleep, and sometimes psychosomatic illnesses when we suffer a loss. What can we get in return?

If the loss was a business failure, we lost money, time, effort, and perhaps our credit rating. A friend of mine had a boat-building business. One night the volatile resin caught fire and practically exploded through the rest of the plant. There was no chance to save a stick of materials. He was finished. "He lost everything," people said, but they were wrong. He retained his business sense, his willingness to work, and the sympathetic ear of his creditors, who believed in him even though he had suffered such a crushing setback. He gained a new appreciation and understanding of his own personal resources — a knowledge that he could come back from even this kind of devastation. He gained the wisdom to look ahead better next time and insure his business and possessions. He gained a new appreciation of his wife and children's love for him and their willingness to stand by him when he was down. He learned how to operate his reopened business on a shoestring, and he learned that you are never beaten until you say you are beaten.

Ettie Lee's family lost their good name. Her progenitor John D. Lee was executed as the perpetrator of the infamous Mountain Meadows Massacre in southern Utah. Probably because of their guilt feelings from their own grandfathers' participation in the massacre, some people in the town decided that the whole Lee family should pay. The Lees lost their standing in the community and the association of some of their former friends. Little Ettie was often shunned by her schoolmates. She could have taken this loss lying down, but she was not that kind of woman. Instead she demanded repayment in full from life, and she got it. She got it by demanding that life pay her in the coin of empathy and understanding for the troubles of others and an ability to rise above her own problems. With these hard-earned riches she opened the Ettie Lee Boys Schools. She blessed the lives of many young men who felt outcast, as she had. And she gained more than she had surrendered in the losses of her early life.

I lost temporarily the companionship of a beautiful and loving wife and the mother of our children. But I determined I would not make such a heavy investment just to return to where I had been before. I decided I would get good measure for my money, and I have already. I understand the hurts and the loneliness of others in a way I never did before. I see the tentative and temporary nature of this life in which we live. I am drawn closer to eternal life in the hereafter. I see more than I ever did before the need to be anxiously doing good with every moment. I love my wife more deeply now than I did when she was with me. I treasure and thank the Lord for the privilege of having served her clear up to the last teaspoon of water I slipped between her lips and the last priesthood blessing I gave her before she died. These memories are locked forever in my heart and hers, and are a significant milestone in our eternal and celestial marriage. I feel a strength and a unity from our children that was not there before. I have known the love and compassion of friends and family in my time of need. I have a list of my goals in life, which I carry with me all the time. They are arranged in priorities, and the first one is to get myself and my family into the celestial kingdom. In the case of my wife, this goal is on its way toward sure fulfillment. This treasured reward cost me the loss of her companionship for a time, but it has assured me that our relationship will continue in eternity if I am worthy.

There is no loss without some attendant gain. If we look carefully, we can always find it. Since we have already paid the price, we should avail ourselves of the prize.

Chapter 14

Not Pawns but Partners of God

It is easy to feel overwhelmed by the forces of nature, the power of other people, the unseen factors of coincidence, and fate that sometimes seems to dictate our destiny. Why one person suffers a loss, while another in similar circumstances seems to escape unscathed, is a question that has baffled observers of the human scene for as long as they have been observing. Some losses seem traceable to a cause: indulging in riotous living and imbibing detrimental substances, for example, will usually result in a loss of health. Even here, however, there are puzzling exceptions— centenarians who swear by a stiff drink or a strong cigar every day, and health-conscious people who die young or live with physical disabilities.

A friend of mine in Long Beach, California, has a beautiful home, a large boat docked at his backyard, a very comfortable standard of living, and a small manufacturing business. He has it all not because of his business, but because he happened to buy a good-sized piece of vacant land several decades ago just about the time the bulging city of Long Beach bulged in his direction.

Dr. Clinton Oaks, professor of business at Brigham Young University, has made a long-term study of students who came through that program and went on to success in the business world. He told me: "They come from all walks of life, all socio-economic strata. They have varied personalities and character traits. Some are outgoing and aggressive. Others are very mild

mannered and introverted. Some have succeeded in small businesses; others with giant corporations. Their personal lives and
habits varied greatly, but all these successful students had one
thing in common—luck. They happened to be in the right place
at the right time.

"Certainly their training was not wasted, and they were prepared to take advantage of the opportunities when those opportunities presented themselves," he observed. But Dr. Oaks is
unusually candid and accurate in his assessment: there is a heavy
dose of luck in every recipe for success.

Even in the area of human relationships, where we have a
fairly high degree of control over our destiny, there seem to be
forces at work beyond our conscious understanding. Some mar-
riages and families seem so much happier than others. Outwardly
they don't appear to be doing that much differently from each
other, but the mixture of past experiences and present personalities
mellows in some relationships and sours in others. Why does luck
seem to smile on some and frown on others? More importantly,
what can we do about it? Nothing, according to some notable
philosophies and religions. The fates have set their faces and
predetermined our destinies. Our only role in the experience is to
enjoy or endure whatever they have decreed for us. This fatalistic
outlook has drawn millions of passive supporters over the ages.
Its disadvantages are obvious: we have no say over our own destiny. But weighed against these are aspects that appeal to the
coward and the quitter in most of us. Under this system we have
no choice, but we also have no responsibility. No one can ever
point the finger at us and say, "You failed." We can pass the
accusation on to the environment, coincidence, or fate.

This denial of responsibility for our own actions pops out in
many curious situations. Recent research has shown a strong
correlation between our mental and emotional states and our
physical health. From the common cold to such dread scourges
as cancer, there appears to be a psychosomatic element. We can,
in a measure, think ourselves to health or sickness. Most of us
have suspected that was the case for a long time. Some people

seem to have both healthy minds and robust bodies, while others, as the saying goes, "enjoy poor health." This is not to say that every disease and disability can be cured by thinking happy thoughts. But the evidence is conclusive that the will to live and an unconquerable spirit send messages to our brain. The brain then dispenses exotic chemicals like interferon and interlukin II. Interferon is a pain- and stress-relieving chemical. Interlukin II triggers the body's immune system and bacteria- and virus-fighting capabilities. This would seem to be good news for everybody. You and I have an arsenal of weapons against the loss of good health built within us as standard equipment. We just need to exercise our will, our faith, and our optimism to activate it. Seems simple enough.

Yet when some of these findings were reported in the distinguished *New England Journal of Medicine,* probably the most respected medical journal in America, there was an outcry of opposition. It centered on the unsympathetic and uncharitable ramifications of this approach to healing. "These people are already dying of cancer or some other disease, and now you want to lay a guilt trip on them in addition to that by telling them their illness is their own fault," came the cry. That line of reasoning sounds humane on the surface, but it can be truly destructive as it eats its way into our spirit. The implications of that statement are best seen by looking at its opposite: that is to say that we have no control over our health, that we are totally at the mercy of medical practitioners, drug dispensers, and coincidence. It leaves the patient powerless.

The truth of the matter is that we are deeply indebted to fine doctors. We are grateful for miracle drugs and medical advances, but we also have a strong personal input into the equation of our own health and sickness. We are "capacitated," as the philosophers term it, in this realm of our lives.

The same philosophy describes every aspect of our lives. We are not autonomous and unaffected by the world around us and the will of God, but we can have input that will affect the outcome. I believe that the Lord does not expect us to be bowed down. He does not want us to be craven cowards, cringing in anticipation of the next blow that may fall on us. I don't believe he is pleased with the kind of defeatism that sometimes passes for humility and obedience, when we lie beaten down by life's losses and say, "It is the will of God that I am lying here, and I will lie here until the will of God picks me up." We are capacitated. We have been given a minute portion of the power of God and charged with the stewardship to use it. We may be so weakened and exhausted by life's losses and tribulations that we can barely move our lips in pleading and prayer, but at least that much we can do with our own power. The Prophet Joseph Smith quoted Christ's parable of the unjust judge who would not respond to the widow's importunings in the night. But she persisted until he was moved to grant her request. Joseph counseled the Saints to follow her example. He said, "Weary the Lord until he blesses you." So long as we have life, we can at least exercise that much power and faith on our own behalf.

But generally we can do much more than just weary the Lord. We can use our own physical, mental, emotional, and spiritual strength to recover from a loss. We can, as the saying goes, work as though everything depended on us and pray as though everything depended on God. Such a combination of our limited power and God's omnipotence and wisdom is the most powerful force in the universe. It will help us to avoid unnecessary losses in our lives and to recover from the necessary losses that will inevitably come to us.

Chapter 15

A More Sure Word

· ·

"I could show you the exact spot in the road," Don Wood said to me. That spot in the road is in southern Idaho between Portland, Oregon, and Provo, Utah. It is as sacred to Don Wood as the place on the road to Damascus was to the Apostle Paul, as sacred as the road to Emmaus was to the disciples of Jesus after he met them there following his resurrection, as sacred as the roadside in Zarahemla was to Alma the Younger and the sons of Mosiah when they met an angel of the Lord there who changed their lives forever. My friend Don was weaving down that highway a number of years ago so blinded by tears and racked by grief that he could barely keep his car on the road. He was on his way to make funeral arrangements for his daughter and her husband and the husband of another daughter, who had all been killed in an airplane crash.

Don Wood is one of the Lord's gallant warriors, a pillar in the priesthood. He had served in a stake presidency and had been a dynamic mission president. He chose a career in medical research so that he might alleviate the sufferings of his fellow human beings. His testimony and spiritual strength had lifted the lives of thousands, but none of us are impervious to pain when it pierces to our innermost heart and soul. To Don and Geneal Wood, their lovely daughters and fine sons were second in their hearts only to the Lord Jesus Christ himself. Nothing could have wrenched their emotional equilibrium like losing one of them, to say nothing of the simultaneous death of three. In addition to the loss of these three precious people, Don's daughter was six months pregnant with his first grandchild. And his good friend, the father of his daughter's husband, was at the controls when the plane malfunctioned. All were killed in the crash. Don was hurting as badly as a man can hurt.

"O God, please help me to do what I need to do. Help me to survive this and be strong," he prayed as he peered through his misty eyes at the outlines of the road before him. "I had prayed such prayers before," he said. "I had received some comfort, but I was still in agony. At that moment I felt a sweet peace descend on me. The tightness I felt in my chest and heart relaxed. I was able to stop sobbing and dry my eyes. The gray feeling that had surrounded me began to dissipate, and I felt comforted and almost joyful. I felt for the first time that this was not a terrible accident that just happened by chance. These wonderful young people were trying their best to keep the Lord's commandments. If a sparrow cannot fall to the earth without his noticing, surely these, his sweet children, could not fall from the sky unnoticed by him. These feelings and thoughts replaced the black hole I had been spinning down into. I have never felt that terrible grief again, and I understand more than I did about the Second Comforter," he told me.

Don took care of the funeral rites for his children and returned to his work in a Catholic hospital. The kind sisters and priests with whom he worked were deeply solicitous of his welfare. They were prepared to pour out sympathy and comfort upon him in his bereavement. They were surprised when instead he comforted them. They had known and loved the family and were likewise suffering grief. He was able to lift their spirits.

"They said they were amazed at how strong I was. I told them not to be impressed with me—I was weak as a wet dishrag—but to know that God had heard my prayers in my deepest hour of need and had answered them. They understood," Don said to me.

In one of the Apostle Peter's letters, he describes to the saints of his day his experiences with Jesus. He tells of how he walked and talked with the Lord. Surely, they must have said to themselves, as we would, "What a fortunate man Peter is to have had that rare opportunity. If I had been there with Jesus and the apostles, I too might know as surely as Peter does of the life, death, and resurrection of Jesus and of the promise that he gives to all of us of life after death." Peter may have sensed the direction of their reasoning, for he continued, "We have also a more sure word of prophecy." (2 Peter 1:19.) If we cross-reference this statement with one from the Prophet Joseph Smith, we learn what Peter meant by "prophecy." The Prophet Joseph said, "The testimony of Jesus is the spirit of prophecy." It would seem correct, then, to interpret Peter's words as saying that he had a more sure testimony, or a more sure knowledge of Christ, than even his senses had given him when he had walked and talked with Jesus and touched him. The Lord told the Prophet Joseph that the more sure word of prophecy meant a man's knowing that he would have eternal life. (See D&C 131:5.)

There may be other ramifications to this intriguing statement by Peter. Theologians have been debating it for almost two millennia. But whatever the statement means, it seems to include a promise from Peter to all who may read his words that the source of his knowledge of Jesus is not primarily his past experiences with the Christ. Rather, the conduit of communication by which he received his knowledge is still open, and all are invited to tap into that conduit and receive the message for themselves.

This principle is certainly appropriate in the dealings of a just God and Father with all his children. If he limited the saving knowledge of Christ to only that tiny handful of people who knew him in mortality, his would be a biased and selective salvation indeed. Furthermore, we would have no responsibility to learn of the Savior and his gospel and to work out our own salvation, because there would be no way to do so. But because he is a just Father and loves all his children equally, and because we do, in fact, have a responsibility to seek out our salvation, he has provided a way for us to know truth from error and to know the greatest of all truths in this life—that life is eternal.

As we partake of the more sure word of prophecy, we know more and more surely of the reality, the divinity, and the mission of Jesus Christ. As we know this, we know that life is eternal, and we glimpse the purpose, the conditions, and the nature of that eternal life. Jesus prayed for his own apostles, shortly before he left them, that they might have this knowledge. He said, "And this is life eternal, that they might know thee the only true God, and Jesus Christ, whom thou hast sent." (John 17:3.)

This knowledge is imperative if we are to overcome the losses in our lives. If a person gives the best years of his life to a goodly work only to see it crumble, or fail, or go unappreciated, how can he be consoled except by considering his efforts another step in his progress through eternity? If one longs for peace, beauty, order, justice, and love in the world, but sees in its blood-soaked history and current conflicts much of the opposite, how can he have hope unless there is a better world yet to come? If one loses the love and companionship of those who make this life worth living, is there ultimately no overcoming unless death itself is conquered? The Apostle Paul wrote, "If in this life only we have hope in Christ, we are of all men most miserable." (1 Corinthians 15:19.) He is right, for we would have tasted the sweetest fruits this life has to offer and then had them snatched from us forever. Better to have lived in ignorance of such joys than to endure the apprehension that they would soon be lost, and the misery when they were gone.

By gaining the "more sure word of prophecy" available to us, we can know in fact that no loss in life is unreclaimable. What is this sure word that is so vital to our overcoming losses in our lives, and how do we obtain it? Perhaps it can be better understood if we compare it to the unsure words through which we gain much of our knowledge. The most respected means of gaining knowledge today is the scientific method. Basically, it consists of setting up experiments or of making observations and then recording the information as objectively as possible. We tend to put great stock in the scientific method of gaining knowledge, and to be suspicious of any avenue outside the five senses. Our suspicion is understandable. Mystics, charlatans, fakes, and deluded spiritualists have plagued mankind throughout recorded history. They come in many forms with many messages and varying degrees of sincerity, but they usually have two things in common: their knowledge and the means by which they gained it cannot be tested by others, and they would have us take their word of knowledge instead of gaining knowledge for ourselves. This nondemonstrable, nonobjective, nonscientific word of knowledge is rightly looked upon with great suspicion by thinking people. The only test we can have for its truth is the reputation of the person who gives it to us.

Less suspect, but equally unsubstantial, are trances, dreams, hallucinations, hunches, flights of fancy, and fortune-telling, through which some people claim to gain knowledge for their own lives. These are less suspect because the people are not trying to control the lives of others, but they are still hard to accept because the experience cannot be repeated or evaluated by others. There are remarkable instances of people gaining apparently accurate insights and truthful information for their lives through these means, however. Many successful people use these systems. If you question them closely as to why they did this thing instead of that, they often say, "I gathered all the information I could, but even then I wasn't sure; so I did what I felt was best under the circumstances." They talk about going with their "gut response," "acting on a hunch," "following intuition." Much of the game of life is played by these rules. In fact, as Oliver Wendell Holmes said, "The art of life is to make correct decisions with inadequate data." Usually there is not sufficient objective data available to make us 100 percent sure that we are making the correct decision. Conclusive data is just that: data that comes in at the conclusion. It is information on the outcome of our decisions and actions. It doesn't come in until we have made the decision.

So, despite our misgivings and the disdain of science, the fact is that much of our knowledge in life comes through nonscientific, nonobjective, nonempirical methods. We can't change that aspect of our human condition; the best we can do is try to understand it and make the best uses we can of those sources of information.

I like the story of the scientist in his laboratory who had a horseshoe nailed over the door. One of his learned colleagues was shocked at this primitive superstition. He blurted out, "Doctor, surely you don't believe that a horseshoe nailed over your door will bring you luck?"

The scientist replied, "Of course not. But I understand it will bring you luck even if you don't believe."

To summarize, the intuitive method of gaining knowledge is not the "more sure word," although it can be useful to us.

Let's now focus on the scientific method. Questioning the scientific method is heresy in our day, when science is the most widely practiced religion in the world. The high priests of science issue their edicts with a finality that must make even the pope envious. We, the untutored masses, usually take their decrees as doctrine chiseled in stone, inscribed with the finger of final authority. They, after all, are the experts in their fields, and we are the unlearned. The only time we get suspicious is when these learned divines differ in their opinions, argue, and even try to excommunicate one another from the faith.

I don't wish to belittle the contributions of the scientific method. It is far better than the system it replaced — the system of superstition and theological fiat. But even at its best the scientific method is a human invention subject to the imperfections of human beings. Scientists can be as dogged in their dogma as any religious zealot. If you don't believe me, try treating the theory of evolution as merely a theory in discussions with most biologists. Try discussing man's potential for godhood with most psychologists and sociologists. Analyze the hand of God in history with most historians. And try to factor the Creator of the cosmos into your equations with most astrophysicists. Much of what we need to know remains to be discovered, and good scientific theories, experiments, and empirical reasoning are marvelous. But skepticism ought not be reserved only for nonscientific modes of seeking knowledge. Scientific tools such as objective observation, hypothetical and theoretical inferences, quantitative measurements, repetition of experiments, peer judgments, and other techniques are useful. But they are not reliable enough for us to trust them to answer the most important questions in our lives.

This is part of what Peter was telling the people of his day. He had gathered impressive evidence of the Christ. He had used his five senses in scientifically respectable ways. He had listened to the first accounts of Christ's resurrection with a skepticism worthy of a scientific board of review. He had seen, heard, and touched the mortal Christ, and the resurrected Christ. Yet he claimed to have a more sure knowledge than he had gained from those experiences, and he promised his listeners that they too could have that knowledge. For Peter knew that his senses could be deceived. Hallucinations, fabrications and falsifications, wishful and wistful thinking—all were as common then as they are today. As Paul wrote, in this life "we see through a glass, darkly." (1 Corinthians 13:12.)

Left to our own resources, we blindly grope through a gray mist of ignorance, feeling for outlines and clues in our quest for knowledge. The Lord knows our vast limitations, and as a loving Father does not want his children to stumble along in ignorance. So he provided for us a "more sure word." To answer the most important questions of our lives, we can hear this word by humbly asking for it. It will tell us the truths we need to know and guide us in overcoming the losses we will experience.

It does not take extensive theological training or long church experience to receive knowledge from God. It takes only two things: a humble request to know and a commitment to believe and act on the knowledge we receive. One of the most powerful prayers in scripture was uttered by and answered to a man who was not even sure God existed. The Book of Mormon tells of the king of all the Lamanites, who had just received his first missionary discussion from Aaron, the son of Mosiah. As every effective missionary does, Aaron bore his own testimony and then counseled the king to pray that he might know the truth of the words he had just heard. The king began his prayer with less than inspiring faith, but with admirable honesty and humility. He prayed, "O God, . . . if there is a God, and if thou art God, wilt thou make thyself known unto me, and I will give away all my sins to know thee." (Alma 22:18.) He was immediately struck with such spiritual power as to render him unconscious. We may not receive such a dramatic manifestation as this, but we can be assured that as we pray with humility and sincerity, we will receive an answer. The comfort and testimony we need to get through our loss will be given to us.

In his final general conference address before his death, Elder Bruce R. McConkie of the Council of the Twelve testified that even when he met his Savior face to face, he would not know any more surely then than he did now that Jesus Christ lives and is our Savior. That same sure testimony of the Christ, that same sure word of prophecy, is available to each of us. As we seek it, so it shall be given, according to our needs.

Chapter 16

Bend or Break

· ·

A few years ago I was rolling across Kansas in an old bus we had refitted to carry the traveling entertainment trio I was part of. The afternoon was warm, calm, and sunny. The freeway was new and smooth, and the country was as flat as the top of a pool table. It was a day for comfortable cruising. Suddenly, I heard a loud, metallic snap, then a screeching, whining sound. The steering wheel in my hand wrenched to the right, and the bus headed straight for the borrow pit. I wrestled it to a stop by the side of the freeway, got out, and looked underneath. A long leaf on the right rear mainspring had snapped and dropped the frame down onto the axle and the wheel. We jacked, blocked and tackled, chained, and prayed the thing together. We limped all the way to Atlanta, Georgia, arriving just in time to do our show.

I later asked the mechanic who fixed it, "What happened?" We had experienced mechanical breakdowns before, but there had always seemed to be a cause. We might have hit a big chuck hole, for instance, or neglected to replace a worn tire, or gradually burned a valve that needed to be replaced. But why would a perfectly healthy spring on a perfectly smooth road on a perfectly lovely day suddenly snap in two? "Metal fatigue," he said. "This spring was built to take only so many flexes. When it has done that, she's done."

My friend Don Budge, a civil engineer, tells me the same thing about roads. Parts of the freeway between Provo and Salt Lake

City were beginning to break up after years of wear. I said, "It seems to me they should go on forever."

He said, "No, they are constructed to carry just so much tonnage. When enough vehicles roll over them to total up that tonnage, they will begin to break down and need to be repaired." The same principle holds true for virtually all mechanical things. Disconcerting as it may seem, those shiny, brand-new automobiles for which people pay a small fortune are beginning to fall apart even as they are driven off the showroom floor.

On the other hand, live things grow stronger through opposition and resistance. I don't know what the difference is between so-called "live" and "dead" materials. Molecules, electrons, and neutrinos are inorganic, but they appear to be some of the liveliest things in the universe. So I guess this demarcation between life and death is as good as any other (at least it is useful for our discussion here): dead things get weaker as they work through difficulties; live things get stronger.

When I was a senior in high school, I remember struggling to do three push-ups. Today, far beyond my physical prime of life, I do a daily sixty or so. The strength has come through years of struggling against resistance. If my muscles were not alive, I guess they would be suffering metal fatigue, and my arms would fall off one morning. There have been mornings when they felt as if they would, but so far it hasn't happened. Now, of course, as I grow older those push-ups will be harder to sustain. The body does grow weaker with age. But the growing strength will still take place in the realms of the mind and the spirit, and in character development. Furthermore, even the slowing down and slackening of physical strength is only temporary. The fading senses and feeble limbs will rise eternally reinvigorated in the resurrection. I believe the strength, skills, and abilities we develop here will be useful then. Certainly, willpower and control over the body's natural appetites and inertia are physical skills worth developing.

The living mind likewise grows by pushing through resistance. I once heard a highly educated man speak of a saying that is sometimes bandied about, "Learning is fun." The man commented, "When people say this, I can only think that either they have never really learned or they have never really had fun." This is true. Learning is satisfying, fulfilling, even joyful, but it is heavier than fun. It is pushing through the fog, constantly refurbishing the memory as it goes blank, straining to understand new concepts and new connections. It is a growing and strengthening exercise.

Recent research indicates that the brain itself may literally grow in size as learning takes place. Dr. Marian Diamond and her fellow researchers at the University of California at Berkeley found this phenomenon in rats, at least. As the rats participated in learning activities such as mazes and rewarded selections, their brains grew and got heavier. They did not add additional neurons (brain cells), but the interconnections between the cells grew and strengthened. Again, this is living matter growing and becoming stronger by overcoming resistance. You could drag a computer, even the big CRAY—the most powerful computer presently in the world—through mazes from now through the Millennium, and its memory chips would not grow the way yours and mine do. Living and nonliving things come out of work and struggle differently. The living things come out stronger; the nonliving things come out weaker.

It has been said that a mind stretched to encompass a new concept or idea never again returns to its former size. From all we can tell, the mind is in an eternal growth pattern. There may be a brief interlude during the final years of this physical existence when the recall functions of the brain may be rendered temporarily less functional. Disease or injury may have similar effects, but these physical impairments will pass and the mind will continue its eternal journey of growth and development. Eventually, we shall comprehend all the mysteries of God, all the knowledge and wisdom of all the universes. We shall comprehend facts, principles, logic, and science; besides these, we shall also comprehend all aesthetics, all subtleties and beauties. We shall understand and empathize with all the feelings of every creature. We shall understand the inner workings of energy and matter and the macrocosmos where edges and borders do not exist. We shall fathom

the eternal past and the eternal future—the beginningless beginnings and endless endings. These concepts are beyond our present
comprehension. Brigham Young said, "When I receive my body
again, shall I cease my learnings? No, I shall then learn a thousand
times more in a thousand times less time."

This is our destiny as living creatures, as eternal intelligences,
and as children of God. If there was a time we could have chosen
otherwise, it has long since passed. We are locked into life. We
could commit suicide, but that would not stop our life. It would
only transfer us to another sphere of existence. Apparently, the
process of making progress is more difficult if we have not done
the things we came here to do. We can commit spiritual suicide
by choosing to follow Satan, but this will merely relegate us to
realms of darkness. Our progress there will apparently be damned,
but we will go on living. Our minds, our spirits, and even our
bodies are eternal, and we cannot will it otherwise.

We can try to take what would appear to be the course of
least resistance and imitate the inorganic world by growing weaker
with each forced flex of our inner springs, as the old bus did. But
in the long run, I think we will find this the harder course because
it is not natural to us. As living things, our instinctive response
is to grow stronger by overcoming obstacles and wading through
resistance. We will do well to follow that natural tendency as we
turn our losses into mental, emotional, and spiritual isometric
exercises in our program of eternal growth.

Chapter 17

Lessons Not to Learn from Loss

Gerald was a teenager when his parents got divorced. There is no easy divorce—at least not for the children. This one was as grisly as usual. Love between the two most important people in Gerald's life gradually turned to apathy, then to suspicion and distrust, and finally to dislike and maybe hatred. It tore him up. The sympathy he received from his peers, teachers, church advisors, and extended family members was well-intentioned, but less than helpful. It wasn't the sympathizers' fault, particularly. The problem developed because of the way Gerald read the messages he was getting from the outside world. To him they said that he was a special case. He had been put upon unfairly by his parents, by the world in general, and by God. He had suffered more than most, and therefore the Lord, the world, and whoever crossed his path owed him something.

Gerald made it his life's work to collect on that debt. If there were household chores and duties to be done, they could be done by others, because Gerald had already suffered enough. If there was homework assigned in school, it couldn't apply to him because his home had been torn apart. The priesthood and church assignments that would normally have fallen on him as an active member would now have to be done by others because God had already asked too much of him.

Before long the trials of life itself—the daily drudgeries and frequent frustrations that are the common lot of all mankind—

were an unfair burden, in his opinion. So he tried to escape these through drinking and drugs. Gerald suffered a terrible loss in the breakup of his parents' marriage, no question about that. But by choosing to react to his loss the way he did, he magnified and personalized that tragedy until it took over his whole life. Within a few years, it cost him his life.

"For whatsoever ye sow, that shall ye also reap." (D&C 6:33.)

"If the Son therefore shall make you free, ye shall be free indeed." (John 8:36.)

"Well done, thou good and faithful servant: thou hast been faithful over a few things, I will make thee ruler over many things." (Matthew 25:21.)

"And we will prove them herewith, to see if they will do all things whatsoever the Lord their God shall command them." (Abraham 3:25.)

"Verily I say, men should be anxiously engaged in a good cause, and do many things of their own free will, and bring to pass much righteousness." (D&C 58:27.)

The scriptures are replete with declarations that we are the final decision makers about our lives and the direction they go. We will be pushed and prodded, acted upon, and influenced by the conditions we go through in this world. But we will never be overwhelmed or coerced by them, unless we choose to be. In all cases, our own decisions will tip the scales toward righteousness or unrighteousness, toward growth or stagnation, toward salvation or damnation. Nobody can make us do anything in this world that is of eternal consequence. We may be imposed upon, intimidated, even incarcerated. We may be forced to perform some labor. But in matters of the heart and mind—those things that dictate our destinies—we are masters of our own fates. When we give away this free agency, for whatever reason, we bring upon ourselves the most tragic kind of loss.

Victor Frankl has become perhaps the classic study of a man who refused to give up this most basic of human rights—the freedom to decide how he would respond to his environment. Everything else was taken from him by his cruel captors. As a

Jewish intellectual in Nazi Germany, he was a danger to the barbaric philosophy and programs of the Third Reich. They could hardly preach their doctrine of the Teutonic, blond, blue-eyed master race with examples of sensitive and scholarly people like Dr. Frankl in their society, coming from supposedly inferior races. So they chose the simple-minded exercise of brute power that the wicked always do when they get the chance. They murdered Dr. Frankl's family in the gas chambers and incarcerated him in a concentration camp. They stripped from him and his fellow prisoners all outward dignity, made them work under conditions one would not inflict on a draft animal, and tried to reduce them to the subhuman species the Nazi philosophy claimed they were.

It did not work. Frankl bent beneath the whip and the chains; he had no choice. But he refused to let his captors enter his brilliant mind. They could break his body, but they could not break his spirit. They took his precious handwritten notes and drafts for his book and destroyed them. They made him work in the snow in rags and sleep on a hard, cold bed with a thin blanket. They beat his body, gave him slop for his mouth and degraded curses for his ears, and assailed his nostrils with the stench of human filth. But Dr. Frankl built an impenetrable barrier between his mind, heart, and spirit and the suffering his body was enduring. He mentally and spiritually insulated himself from his degrading environment and sadistic guards. He refused to let this evil seep in to canker and rot his soul. He continued to think of the beautiful days with his family and loved ones, to create powerful mental worlds in which his mind and spirit lived while his body suffered. He continued to exercise his mind with profound and infinite thoughts and logic so that it was not distracted totally by the squalor around it. This was not an easy thing; it was a constant battle. But no tyrant has ever invented a mental barbed wire that can enclose the minds of men and women like Victor Frankl.

Frankl was wiser than most. He also did not allow hatred and revenge to rot his mind. He continued to consider his captors as human beings, even though they did not give him the same consideration. Eventually Victor Frankl won his war. The Third Reich was defeated; he never was. When he was released at the end of the war, his notes had been long since destroyed, but his mind had not. With indomitable power, he pulled his ideas together again and wrote a book that has inspired millions, *Man's Search for Meaning*.

Most of us will not find ourselves in the extremes of almost total loss that Victor Frankl did. But no matter what our challenges, our heartbreaks, our setbacks, our losses, we cannot use them as an excuse to cave in, give up, and let outside influences direct our destiny. The examples of Dr. Frankl and others stand as beacons in the darkness of this philosophy. We may choose to draw the window shades of our soul against these beacons, but the light will still pierce the cracks and seep into our inner being. We will know that we have sold our birthright of free agency for the pottage of prisoners and slaves.

On the surface such a trade seems out of the question. Who in his right mind would trade freedom for bondage? But a closer inspection will show us that slavery does indeed have some advantages — or at least some elements that are perceived by some people as advantages. Prisoners do not have to worry where their next meal is coming from or what they will do with their days. They don't have to wonder where they will get money for clothing or necessities. Prisoners needn't ponder and plan about how they can fulfill their responsibilities; they have no responsibilities. Whatever planning is necessary will be done by those over them. Prisoners needn't worry about how to control their appetites and passions. There is little opportunity for them to channel their passions into antisocial acts. They needn't strain their brains on ways to improve their performance or develop new ideas or innovations. If prisoners merely keep their heads down and stay out of trouble, that is generally considered good behavior.

If a person's ultimate goal is security, it's hard to beat the walls and bars and predictability of a well-run prison. "Maximum Security" is about as secure as it gets in this life. If we choose to give our lives over to others, there are many people willing to take them — to relieve us of our burden of self-defined destiny and pay us for it in the coin of security and slavery. And, of course, the prison need not be made of steel and concrete. Very solid prisons can be fashioned of alcohol, drugs, and tobacco. Hobbles for the heart and soul can be fashioned from hatred, envy, and pride. In terms of our discussion here, making excuses, blaming others, disavowing responsibility for our own actions because we have suffered a loss, and other habits weave, strand by strand, a strong tether rope that can stake us to the ground securely and stop our progress in its tracks.

Society today seems largely geared to shifting responsibility. The first response of many people on suffering any kind of setback seems to be not "How can I learn and develop from this loss?" but "Whom can I blame it on?" "Whom can I sue?" "How can I transfer the responsibility for this to somebody else and get money from them?"

I am not suggesting that we ignore issues of legitimate liability on the part of people who may be responsible for our loss. I'm talking about the reckless and random litigation of our day, which has been called "the age of the suers." This kind of action, no matter how much money the complainer and his lawyer end up with, is a step into slavery.

America's genius for technological innovation and invention is in jeopardy today. One of the reasons is that people demand that every new product or technique be 100 percent safe. Any loss is immediately blamed on the inventor or the innovator. This chilling climate is not conducive to new ideas and progress. Safety and security become the highest priorities.

We all lived in a safe society at one time. There was no sickness; there were no setbacks. There was no danger, no death, and no loss. But there was also no progress beyond a certain point. So a council was called to decide how to help the people of that realm continue their progression. One of the leaders at that council attempted to sell a program of total security, which is merely a synonym for slavery. He said, "I will take these spirits down to an earth, run them through their exercises, and force them to return. Not one soul shall be lost, and because I shall do it, I shall receive all the glory." On its own terms that was a fair arrangement. If he was to make all the decisions and accept all the responsibility, he probably deserved whatever glory was given in the end. One-third of the millions of people at the council felt so disposed and followed him.

But then arose the Savior of mankind and, on behalf of his brothers and sisters, upheld the Father's plan. He explained that we would take responsibility for our own acts. When we stumbled and sinned, he would pay the price for us by the sacrifice of his own godly life. Those under this program would be free to choose good or evil and would take the responsibility for their choices and the actions that followed them. They would make mistakes, but if they called upon his name, repented of their sins, and did all in their power to make things right, he would make up the difference. In this program the Christ said he would not take the glory but would give the glory unto the Father. And what is this glory? "This is my work and my glory—to bring to pass the immortality and eternal life of man," the Lord said. (Moses 1:39.)

It is not in the hollow shouting of hallelujahs that God is glorified, but in the growth, perfection, immortality, and eternal life of his children. When we shift responsibility for our lives to anyone else because of losses we may suffer (or for any other reason), we block our own progress, and we deny to God the glory that would rightly be his through our growth. The healthy and proper response to loss is to renew our efforts and exertions to endure its pain, overcome its problems, and use the strength we derive to continue our progress toward godhood.

Traveling Tips

Here are some suggested steps to help you move through the third phase of your journey in overcoming your loss:

Bring strength into your mind and spirit by reading biographies of people who have overcome obstacles. There may be a tendency to compare their problems with yours, but try to avoid this. It can be discouraging to feel that they overcame huge problems while you are still struggling to come back from apparently smaller ones. It is not useful to compare people—a bracing challenge for one might be an almost overwhelming task to someone else. The reason for reading these life stories is not to compare but to take strength from other people's struggles and tips from their techniques.

Build your strength by doing something difficult every day. Then be sure to reward yourself for having done it. Some people describe this as doing something hard and something easy every day. I was speaking to a group on this subject once, and a man came up afterwards and enthusiastically said, "I do that. I do something hard and something easy every day. The hard thing I do is to get out of bed; the easy thing I do is to go back to bed." He had the principle down, I guess, but a little more imagination might have enriched his program.

Physical therapists say not to put too much strain on a muscle that is already in tension. A little bit of additional pressure can gradually build up the muscle strength, but too much while the muscle is under stress can do damage. The same principle applies in times of loss. Don't try to move any mountains; just scoop a shovelful or two and then reward yourself for the additional effort. A little bit of progress on cleaning your home or yard, doing part of a project you have been meaning to get to, writing your personal history, or helping a neighbor—these additional efforts in your life can pay marvelous dividends in developing the strength you need to overcome your loss.

Expand the number and the use of optimistic words in your vocabulary and limit the negative ones. Jesus said that we would be judged by every word that comes out of our mouths. Part of that judgment will come in the last days, when those who are affected by our words offer testimony, and the Great Judge of us all makes his decisions. But a big part of that judgment is occurring every day—not by others, but by ourselves. We hear our own words, and our unconscious mind reacts to them by trying to fulfill the prophecies we have promised in our words. If we say we are doing fine, our unconscious mind tries to make that the case. If we say things are looking up, our mind takes this as a cue and finds evidence to prove that point. And, of course, the opposite is also true. If we deal in negatives, our mind will search for ways to make them come to pass. Some people have succeeded in changing their negative thought patterns by putting an elastic band on their wrist. Whenever they slip and say something negative, they say, "Stop it," and snap the band against their wrist. I personally prefer rewards for good behavior over punishment for mistakes, but this is an effective way to call attention to negative words and mental sets that may be draining your strength.

Feel free to let your mind go back to the good times before your loss. There is nothing hidden or forbidden back there, and the sooner your mind finds that out, the less it will be piqued by curiosity and constantly wanting to return to that time.

Practice taking control of your body. Try the relaxation tech-

nique mentioned earlier in this book of tensing and then relaxing all the muscle groups in your body. Now, in this relaxed state, say to yourself a word—perhaps the word "relax" itself. Associate this word with your present physical feelings of relaxation and rest. Practice this until merely the suggestion of the word can bring about this relaxed state of your body. Then in the future as you feel the tension and fear that sometimes come with loss, say to yourself, "Relax," and remember this quiet, peaceful, and pleasant state you are in right now.

Mental control can also help on the opposite end of the spectrum, when your body is so groggy and lazy it won't respond. Practice having your mind tell a muscle to move, and then consciously move it. Fasting for a day is a great help in developing these powers of the mind.

Look back at how far you have come, how much you have already endured, and take confidence and solace from it.

Study the plan of salvation and consider it anew from its beginningless beginnings to its endless end in light of your new condition of loss.

Look for true symbolism and metaphor in the world about you. Often plants and animal species lose certain traits and even members of their kind in order to strengthen the strain and help them focus and survive. Sometimes we need to drop certain activities or possessions in order to help us better focus on the truly important things in our lives.

Notice your own physical, mental, and emotional growth. It has always come through struggle and frequently through pain. If we did not put some stress on our systems, they would never grow. That seems to be an immutable law of life.

Make a list of the character attributes in which you are now stronger because of your loss. Make a list of those in which you are not now stronger but could become stronger because of your loss. These could include such traits as understanding, empathy, *perseverance, courage. These can all be strengthened because of what you have gone through and overcome.*

Set out a one-thousand-year goal plan. We talk of eternity, but most of us have time on our hands after a few hours or a few days on our own resources. Eternity is truly beyond our comprehension, but a thousand years is encompassed in world history. So ask yourself, what things would you be doing now to accomplish goals sometime within the next millennium? Not many people think this way, although it is a very productive exercise. But having gone through a period of loss and reevaluation, you will find this a good time to strengthen your planning and goal-setting ability.

Part of the productivity of thinking in such a long perspective is the "intimations of immortality" it gives us, to borrow the title of William Wordsworth's poem. The longer we can stretch our perspective, the more our present big and little losses and setbacks assume their proper importance. They are important, in that they help to set our direction and mold our character. But they are not the ultimate determinants of our destiny. We can overcome them and use them as stepping stones on our upward, eternal journey toward godhood and complete happiness.

Part 4

The Value of Loss in Our Lives

The Value of Loss

....

The hardest concept for most of us to grasp and hold in times of loss is this: Loss is an indispensable part of life and growth. When we remember this, it makes our loss much easier to bear. But it is hard to remember and appreciate this principle when we are hurting.

I have included these additional essays to help us strengthen our conviction of this concept and take comfort from it.

Chapter 18

Temporary Loss, Eternal Gain
. . . .

I was once fighting forest fires in the Hell's Canyon area of
Idaho. We were exhausted from fighting one fire and were trying
to catch a few winks of sleep on the bus taking us to the next
fire. We hoped it would not be as rugged a climb as the last one.
The bus stopped, and we all looked out the windows. We were
heartened to see that the fire was only a few miles away on the
face of the mountain. But then we got off the bus, walked to the
edge of the road, and groaned. The fire was close, all right, but
between us and it lay a deep canyon that dropped clear to the
Salmon River. We would have to descend for miles through un-
derbrush and then climb back up again to get to our destination.
Forest fires don't wait. There was no alternative but to grab our
tools and our packs and set off. Soon we were in dense growth
and could not see much of where we had been or where we were
going. But we did know one thing—every step was taking us down.
We were losing altitude that we would later have to regain by
puffing up the other side of the canyon. We did have one advantage:
we had seen the big picture. We knew where we were heading,
and that if we persevered we would eventually regain this lost
altitude and arrive at our destination.

Life is sometimes like that. We know that the ultimate direction for man is upward, eternally upward—that the goal is
godhood. But sometimes, encompassed about by the undergrowth,
weeds, and trees of this temporary world situation, we can lose

track of where we are going, particularly if we seem to be losing ground with every step, or if we fall off a cliff and lie bruised and bleeding at the bottom.

This life is full of strange and devious paths that can lead us astray. Evil can sometimes appear to be good. Long-term failure can disguise itself as temporary success. Even the principle of growth and development can be twisted into a cruel practical joke by life. Just ask Richard and Maile Rowley. They, like all good parents, longed to see their baby son grow, and grow he did. But then they found out at what a terrible cost. For as his arms and legs and then his trunk began to stretch out, they created the equivalent of bare wires along his nervous system. Normally, there is a myelin shield that protects and insulates the nerves and keeps their messages traveling along the tracks to the voluntary muscles. Their son had had such a shield over his nerves perfectly intact when he was born. His mother's body had created the material for that shield and put it safely in place for her baby. But for some reason unknown to science, David's body did not continue to extend the shield. His growing limbs soon broke through the original covering he started out with as a baby and exposed the open nerves. Richard and Maile waited anxiously for him to begin walking. A little late, he did, but there was something not quite right about his walk. Instead of growing stronger and more co-ordinated as he grew, he seemed to be experiencing the opposite. The longer and larger his limbs, his neck, and then his trunk grew, the weaker and more useless they became.

For eleven years Richard and Maile sought out the best medical minds of the country for an answer to this cruel double-cross on the principle of growth. Doctors guessed polio, multiple sclerosis, and Lou Gehrig's disease of creeping paralysis. Finally, at the Mayo Clinic they discovered the correct diagnosis—the degenerating myelin shield on his nerves. But there was nothing they could do. For another eleven long years, Richard and Maile prayed and watched their son's unconquerable spirit fight a losing battle against the enemy within. David never quit. On crutches, in braces, in a wheelchair, and finally confined to his bed, he battled on. His mind stood out in stark contrast to his body. It continued to grow stronger as his body grew weaker. He graduated from high school and college and enrolled in post-graduate studies. By then he needed a brace just to hold his head up, and he tapped out his lessons with a pencil held in his teeth.

One day David called his family and his close friends about him. He laughed and joked with each one of them. Then he gave each one a long and loving look. He breathed out one last gentle breath and was dead. Richard was deeply grieved, but Maile was inconsolable. "Why? Why in those years would God not answer our prayers?" she cried. "If there is a God, why can't he, or why won't he, help us?" Every day for three months Richard took his heartbroken wife to David's grave, where she poured out again and again her questions and her grief.

There was apparently no answer. David's earthly progress had been into paralysis. His forward steps had been ever downward, and finally into death. Little by little he had lost his powers, and finally lost life itself — or so it seemed to his sorrowing mother. With a pierced heart that only a mother can feel at the death of her child, Maile wept over her son's tombstone even as Mary wept at the base of the cross bearing her crucified son.

But then one morning in the third month, David's voice came into his mother's mind at the grave. He said, "Mother, don't grieve. I am well. I came to the earth to receive a body, and I received one. I came to increase my knowledge and intelligence. This I have done. Now I have taken the next step in my journey. I am learning and growing in knowledge and wisdom. I am happy. Please let me see you be happy too."

Maile got up from her knees a new woman. She saw a beautiful world around her. She took the hand of her strong and loving husband, and they went home in peace at last. David was not dead. His life was not a tragedy. His creeping paralysis had not been a slow descent into death, but another way of making progress upward into life eternal. He had, in a sense, gone downhill, even as we had descended the mountain in pursuit of the forest fire. But he, like us, had been pursuing a goal. The temporary trees and brush of this life had obscured the goal for a time in Maile's eyes, but now she too saw it clearly. This knowledge of the journey we are making and of our ultimate destination makes loss in this life bearable, and even joyful. Finding joy in loss is not an exercise in masochism. It is a result of gaining the correct perspective on our lives. The longer our view, the more we can put our losses into proper perspective.

There is a steep hill behind our house. On most mornings, I jog up that hill. It is a killer—some mornings an almost insurmountable obstacle. I'm always puffing by the time I get to the top. But I often fly in an airplane over that same hill on my way to a presentation of some kind. From 20,000 feet up, that hill is a piece of cake. It's tucked into the foothills of the mighty Wasatch Range, and I can barely make it out. From the satellite photos of earth I've seen, I can't find my hill at all. It disappears into the topography. Thus it is with the losses in our lives. Standing close to them, we find them almost overwhelming. But placed in the perspective of our eternal journey, they turn from impassable obstacles to stepping stones along our path of progress.

It might be well to review this path called *eternal progression*. Life eternal is directly linked to a correct knowledge of God and his creations. Jesus told his disciples as part of his great, high priestly prayer in the seventeenth chapter of John, "And this is life eternal, that they might know thee the only true God, and Jesus Christ, whom thou hast sent." (John 17:3.)

Several important attributes of God relate to loss in our lives. The first is to know that God is omnipotent. He could protect and insulate us from any loss. He could miraculously snatch us out of harm's way whenever we were threatened. He could preserve the lives of all our loved ones indefinitely. He could whisper to us the right stocks to buy and business moves to make so we could be blessed materially. He could stop harmful bacteria and viruses in their tracks. They are under his control. He could make us strong and physically attractive. He could dry all our tears, or, easier yet, structure our lives so there was never an occasion to cry. He has the power to do all this because he is omnipotent.

But God is also omniscient. He has all knowledge and wisdom. His wisdom tells him that a pampered existence would not be good for his beloved children. We would never grow, develop, and fulfill our potential. So, in his wisdom, he refrains from overprotectiveness lest he limit growth. More than anything, God wants us to become as he is. This is his work and his glory. He knows we have this potential. He inspired his prophet Lorenzo Snow to write, "As man is, God once was. As God is, man may become."

To become gods is our ultimate goal and destiny. This knowledge should inspire us with a greater awareness of our potential. Surely, to attain such a state of exaltation requires a long and exacting training course. We delude ourselves if we expect to attain the character of godhood through shortcuts or quick courses. The lessons of eternal life must be learned one by one. The godlike traits must not only be developed, but also perfected. These traits include those enumerated by the Christ in his immortal Sermon on the Mount and repeated to the Nephites at Bountiful.

"Yea, blessed are the poor in spirit who come unto me, for theirs is the kingdom of heaven. And again, blessed are all they that mourn, for they shall be comforted. And blessed are the meek, for they shall inherit the earth. And blessed are all they who do hunger and thirst after righteousness, for they shall be filled with the Holy Ghost. . . . And blessed are all the pure in heart, for they shall see God." (3 Nephi 12:3–8.)

None of these characteristics, nor the others expounded and exemplified in the Lord's ministry, are cerebral exercises. They are matters of the heart at least as much as the head. They are the challenging curriculum of the academy of life, and they can be learned only by living through the experiences that teach them. Only those who have been touched by poverty of the spirit feel a need to search out the Christ. We can never know the blessings that can come with mourning until we have mourned. Only those who have been tempted by and overcome this world's opportunities for puffing up our pride and coddling our vanity can know the true meaning of meekness. Until we have suffered some sense of spiritual starvation, we are not ready to truly hunger and thirst after righteousness. And until we approach the Lord's table with that depth of hunger, we will never be filled with the Holy Ghost sufficiently to purify our hearts and make us worthy and able to see God. This kind of learning comes only through living.

The Apostle Peter gives a similar curriculum. Like the Beatitudes, and like every effective learning program, the lessons build upon each other. So Peter said, "Add to your faith virtue; and to virtue knowledge; and to knowledge temperance; and to temperance patience; and to patience godliness; and to godliness brotherly kindness; and to brotherly kindness charity." (2 Peter 1:5–7.)

Life's experiences are irreplaceable in learning these lessons and developing and perfecting our characters. They are also indispensable in the second phase of the learning process, which is testing to see whether we have achieved, internalized, and retained the characteristics we were sent here to develop. How can we know whether we have, in fact, acquired the virtue of meekness if we are never tested with the temptation of pride? How shall we know if we have become self-satisfied and ceased to hunger after the spirit of the Lord unless we are constantly faced with the temptation to turn away from him? And as the Book of Mormon often points out, it is not enough to have *obtained* a state of grace in these virtues. We must *retain* that state as well. Alma asked this pointed question: "I say unto you, my brethren, if ye have experienced a change of heart, and if ye have felt to sing the song of redeeming love, I would ask, can ye feel so now?" (Alma 5:26.)

So our lives continue to be a succession of learning experiences, tests, and bracing challenges and opposition to keep us growing, progressing, and moving up that strait and narrow path toward godhood. The degree of incline of the upward path is calibrated to the strength of the pilgrim on it. It is not made easy for any traveler, but neither is it impossible.

But why must this academy of eternal life be a boarding school? Why not some correspondence course we could study while we continue to live in our heavenly home? Parents know at least one of the reasons why. "Hang up your clothes and make your bed. Eat your vegetables and brush your teeth. Say, 'Heavenly

Father, I thank thee for . . . ' " we teach our children when they are tiny. "Make the most of your time and opportunities. Serve others. Search the scriptures. Be faithful in your church duties. Seek the Lord's Spirit and confirmation in all that you do," we counsel them when they are older. In most cases they respond to counsel and guidance and grow into responsible adults. But never, until they leave home, do they, or we, know for certain whether they have internalized the lessons of youth. Only then do the truths come crashing down: if I don't hang up my clothes and do the dishes, no one else will. The car does not automatically fill its tank with gas. To have a friend is to be a friend. I have no special claim on the world's affection, as I did in my family just because of who I am. Anything I truly possess I will have to earn by my own efforts. I am free to do evil or good, but I am not free to escape the consequences of my actions. And the great secret of life: "men are, that they might have joy" (2 Nephi 2:25), and joy comes from obeying the Lord and enduring to the end.

We can never know as children whether we have in fact learned and internalized these truths until we have the independence of action to be tested. The same principle holds true in our relationship with our heavenly parents. Under their direct supervision, it was easy to be good, or at least not bad. But our growth was limited in this greenhouse environment. We needed the bracing challenges of outdoors to test our strength and continue our development, so we are here. A veil has been temporarily drawn between that pre-earthly life and this one, and another veil between this and the life to come. These veils are semipermeable, and messengers do sometimes travel between the premortal, postmortal, and present existences. But we do not associate with immortal beings with the ease and frequency we once knew and will one day know again.

This separation and isolation from our heavenly home and family can be confusing, frightening, and discouraging. The apostles of Jesus had these feelings as he was about to leave them. They had experienced a glimmer of the eternities when they had walked and talked with the Lord. Now they wondered how they could survive without his constant companionship. He consoled them with these words as he left, "And I will pray the Father, and he shall give you another Comforter, that he may abide with you for ever." (John 14:16.)

The other comforter of which the Christ spoke was the third member of the Godhead, the Holy Ghost. His function is to enlighten, strengthen, and comfort us while we are on our earthly journey here, and to guide us back to our heavenly home. The Holy Ghost may not be visible to our earthly eyes, but the effects of his ministry are obvious to all who have their senses attuned to spiritual things. In the case of the apostles, the Holy Spirit turned them from a dispirited and discouraged group of former followers to a courageous quorum of apostles and ambassadors for Jesus Christ. Thereafter, they fearlessly faced and overcame every obstacle, including martyrdom. Nothing in this world could crush their mighty spirits.

And so it can be with us if we follow their example. We can overcome every test and every trial set before us. All our losses can be eventual gains. Losses of the goods and glories of this world will not crush our spirits, for we will see them in their proper perspective. Losses of mobility and mental skills through physical and mental handicaps will not destroy us, for these shall eventually be restored to us. The loss of loved ones will not be inconsolable because we will carry with us the promise of a future reunion followed by an inseparable eternity.

Someday when pain is a thing of the past, we will look back from our heavenly home and understand more perfectly. We will see why losses came to us. Until that time, much of what we know will be whispered to us by the Holy Ghost. When it is in our best interest, he will give us the knowledge we need. When our knowing too much too soon would hinder our eternal progress, that knowledge will be withheld until the proper time. And throughout our journey, the Spirit will whisper comfort to us in our losses and bring us the "peace of God, which passeth all understanding." (Philippians 4:7.)

Chapter 19

Love, Loss, and the Human Predicament

. . . .

For a year the small metal identification plate at the head of the grave read simply "Dayna Harris." There was no headstone. It wasn't a question of expense; Dayna's parents are financially well off. It was a problem of pain. Her parents, and particularly her mother, Joy, had a hard time facing the additional pain that picking out a headstone would bring them.

Joy Harris is aptly named. She loves life and feels it with passion. She loves her husband and her children. When her daughter Dayna died of cancer of the brain, the experience gashed a deep wound in Joy's heart that will be a long time healing. She aches and agonizes over the loss of her daughter more than she would if she were a less loving and less sensitive person. Is her deep loving worth the pain it causes her?

On another street in our town lives a man struggling with the same question. We'll call him Glen. The big cottonwood trees in his front yard tower over the house and protect it from travelers and trespassers. The front windows are small and curtained. There is no welcoming and protecting front porch for visitors—only a doorway cut in the brick facing, with a glass storm door sealing out the elements and the sounds outside and a heavy oak door to protect the privacy within. Few people knock on that intimidating door. Glen has made it known he wants it that way. Inside, he and his wife lead a rather solitary existence. He's not a hermit; he works and gets about town as much as he needs to. But his soul, like his house, is sealed off as much as possible from the rest of humanity.

Many years ago some remarks and actions of others offended Glen. He decided people weren't worth the pain they caused, so he shut most of them out of his life. He will not be stabbed in the heart by the death of a child because he has no children. He won't feel the pain and loss of a friend because he has carefully avoided making emotional commitments to others. His marriage appears to be more an accommodation than a deep love affair. Thus has Glen tried to protect himself from the human predicament.

Philosophers, theologians, and observers from a number of fields have meditated on this predicament. It has been defined from a variety of directions depending on the background of the definer. The most workable definition I have ever read of the human predicament came from Sydney Harris. He said that our problem stems from our human need to love. We must love and be loved or we are something less than human. Yet it is the nature of human life to have those things we love taken from us sooner or later. This is the human predicament.

It has been said that a problem well defined is a problem half solved. Let's look at Harris's definition of the human predicament and see what answers spring from it. Then we'll see if we can add to the definition and thereby find some solutions.

As Harris accurately points out, to be human is to love. We have an inborn tendency to seek out the love and association of each other. Most of what motivates us in life has to do with our relationships with others — everything from desiring the approval of peers to the romantic love that the ballads say makes the world go round; to the deep, altruistic, selfless love in which we try to emulate the fathomless love of Christ. The ancient Greeks had a different word for each of these kinds of love. *Eros* is romantic love; *philos* is the brotherly love in which we hold dear those who are near to us and similar to us in family, culture, habits, or tastes. The highest form of love, *agape*, is the unselfish, godlike love that demands nothing in return, that can love even its enemies, and that seeks only to bless everything with which it comes in contact.

In terms of the human predicament, these definitions are interesting. Most of us are capable of *eros*. We can respond to attractive people who flatter our egos and self-image, and may stir up our hormones. Even the most self-centered people seem capable of responding to this sort of relationship, at least until they grow tired of each other.

The second form of love, *philos*, is likewise not far above our human capabilities. It is not too hard to love those who are like us — whose skin color, religious beliefs, social habits, likes, dislikes, tastes, and place of residence are similar to our own. Birds of a feather do tend to flock together because they easily understand and empathize with one another. There is no great strain in those relationships.

But *agape* is the love that can be smitten on one cheek and immediately turn the other, the love that can "bless them that curse you, do good to them that hate you, and pray for them which despitefully use you, and persecute you." (Matthew 5:44.) This kind of love is a lifetime quest for the best of people. And, interestingly, those who achieve it, or part of it, are those we describe in the most human of terms. We say that such a person is a great human being, a humanitarian, a tribute to the human race. Apparently, the more love we can develop, the more human we are.

And in terms of the human predicament, the more love we develop, the more vulnerable we are to the pain of loss. The person bound up in his own self-love misses most of the joys of this life, but he is in a sense at least a self-contained package. He often seems oblivious to the opinions or the suffering of anyone but himself. The person functioning on the level of brotherly love is vulnerable to the opinions and response of those he has chosen to love, but since he has shut out or disdained most of humanity, he is not easily hurt by what they may or may not do or think about him.

To the person committed to the deep, Christlike love of *agape* — the love that Paul and Moroni call charity — the deepest, richest treasures of the human experience are offered. Likewise, the possibilities for pain are everywhere. No living thing, not even the earth itself, can suffer without this person's suffering also, if he or she is aware of it. The epitome of this love was demonstrated by Christ in the Garden of Gethsemane. Here he felt the pain of the sins of every person who ever lived or ever will live. We are not capable of that depth of love yet. That is humanness taken to its ultimate destiny, which is godhood. But we can and should strive to emulate that Christlike love among one another.

What does that do to the human predicament? It raises the ante to infinite proportions in the game of life. To cut ourselves off from love is to save ourselves from much of the pain of this world, but at the cost of all that makes us truly human. To open ourselves up to love is to make ourselves vulnerable to the deepest pains the human heart can experience – to have those things and people we love ripped from us. Eventually, we are certain it will happen. Either we shall be taken from this life, or they shall. Eventually we will give up our earthly possessions, our youthful vigor, our friends and family. Either we shall die young or watch as even our senses are taken from us and we pass away, as Shakespeare said, "sans [without] teeth, sans eyes, sans taste, sans everything."

The human predicament has no solution in human terms. Some of the frustration and attendant ills of this world result from that fact. We have tried to solve eternal problems from a human, this-world perspective. In politics Karl Marx called religion an opiate and focused his governmental theories on this world alone in materialism. The result for those who have adopted his theories has been an insatiable hunger for land and power. And why not? If materialism is your god, the more wealth you can preside over, the closer you are to your heaven. In our own country we have focused on what we call the good life. We have defined it as more material possessions, more freedom from responsibility, more pleasures and luxuries, fewer constraints. The result has been a terrible loss of the virtues that have always sustained America. We live in a selfish and hedonistic society that would have shocked those who originally defined the government and culture of America. Evaluating our personal lives by the measuring stick of mortality alone has sent us on an endless quest for comforts, youth, physical beauty, sensual gratification, and the satisfying of earthly appetites. When we find that these things are torn from us, we can become bitter at life.

The only answer to the human predicament lies beyond the human condition. We need to understand that it is not the human sphere but heaven that is our ultimate goal and destination—that whatever price we pay in pain to develop deeper love is well worth the sacrifice. Only through such sacrifice do we develop godlike traits. When we understand and practice these things, we see that the predicament is only temporary. It is a test, a training ground for us. Ultimately, all that we have suffered and sacrificed will be worth the price, and those loved ones and loved things we have lost shall be returned to us.

Chapter 20

Competition Creates Losses

My son Benjamin came thundering down the home stretch on his way to winning his sixth-grade cross-country race. "Way to go, Benji! Pour it on! Finish strong!" I shouted from the sidelines. He gave it his best kick for my benefit and burst across the finish line a winner. What did it matter if there were forty-seven winners in front of him?

With a house full of active children, we are always involved in some kind of contest, from the Cub Scout pinewood derby to the state cross-country championship. We win some, and we lose some. I have three standard questions every time one of our children comes from a competition. The questions come in order of importance, and I prefer them answered in order: "Were you a good sport? Did you have a good time? Did you win?" We can always get two out of three—hopefully, the most important first two. Competition in our lives needs to be under control.

I'm convinced that we often suffer loss in our lives unnecessarily because we create competitions where they don't need to exist. Competition generally means that someone will win and someone, usually a lot of someones, will lose. We compete in school, on the job, in social settings, and even in the home. We even try to compete with the forces of nature, the laws of chance, and, I suspect, with the will of the Lord.

Competition has its place in life. It can be stimulating and entertaining to watch people who have prepared themselves mentally or physically for a contest match their skills against one another. Competition may enhance the performance of the competitors and raise the performance standards of the activity in which they are competing. From sandlot baseball games to the Olympics, from an after-dinner game of Chinese checkers to the grand masters' chess tournaments, competition can be a useful diversion.

But contests and competition at any level need to be kept securely within their proper bounds. We should not confuse winning with worth. Some of the saddest stories in sports are of people who have not made that distinction. Inevitably, they found that their speed, strength, and coordination slipped with age, and they were replaced by new champions. If their self-worth was tied with their blue ribbons, they had little left for their life's work. Their confidence faded with the fading cheers of the crowd. We need to remember that running faster, jumping higher, making more touchdowns or baskets, or winning more scholarships, accolades, and honors is not a measure of our success or failure as human beings. Drive, discipline, and setting high standards for ourselves can be very valuable, but the actual winning of plaudits is far too arbitrary and temporary for us to build our foundation upon. These shifting sands are too easily washed away by the winds and waves of chance, coincidence, and public opinion.

This counsel may not apply directly to most of us, since few actually wear the laurel crown of victory. But millions of us these days identify with the competitors. Some people see it as a mark of degeneracy in our culture that twenty-two people play on a football field and fifty thousand sit watching in the stands. The observers' exercise is primarily with the vocal cords to holler and the elbow to stuff hot dogs into the mouth. What kind of comment is it on our culture when some people's greatest claim to self-worth seems to be that a team from a city they happen to live in wins a game?

But there is a more direct way in which the concept of contests affects us all, every day of our lives. That is, we tend to set up competitions and contests where none need to exist. Alfie Kohn, a professor at Tufts University, has written a book titled *No Contest*. He confronts head-on our widely held assumption that competition is the natural order of things in the world. In the minds of many people, this is throwing mom's apple pie on the flag. Every red-blooded American knows that "it's a jungle out there," "survival of the fittest," "nice guys finish last."

It isn't so, according to Kohn's studies. The basis of success in virtually every field of endeavor—human, animal, and plant—is not competition. It is cooperation. Nobody can survive alone, and the more we adopt a philosophy that someone must lose in order for us to win, the more we lose. We bring undue pressure upon ourselves to perform. We alienate those who could help us. We encourage opposition from those who ought not to oppose us. Kohn scores some telling points. Even in the most dog-eat-dog marketing contests in business, people within the organization have to cooperate or they cannot be competitive. The competing businesses have to cooperate or they will soon find themselves facing hostility from government and from their own public. And, at more basic levels, every person must eventually cooperate if this planet is to be habitable. We delude ourselves when we think life is a competition. It is more than anything a cooperation.

The same is true in our personal lives. When we see everything in a competitive mode, it becomes win/lose. For us to win, something or somebody else must lose. To experience the good life, we must gather about us some predetermined or vaguely assumed quantity of possessions. If we don't, we have lost in this contest of life. We see our human relationships as win/lose. For example, if our children don't do what we want them to, they win and we lose. We begin to throw out challenges indiscriminately to the whole environment. We must win over illness, depression, handicaps. Even the cosmos itself can be a battleground if we take this mental set to its furthest extreme. We begin to see ourselves, in a sense, in competition with God himself. If we can just accumulate enough good works, stars on the forehead, and spiritual rewards for work well done, we can win the celestial contest. The prize is the title to a fine mansion and a lovely estate in the eternal realms. On the other hand, if we fall short we will lose in this cosmic competition.

These competitive, win/lose attitudes can wear us down to the nub, especially as we find that we can't win them all. We will also find, as is the case in all competitions, that the ecstasy of victory doesn't compensate for the agony of defeat. I have won a few games and lost a few on the fields of athletic endeavor. I have won some scholarships and failed to reach some academic goals. I have won some fine jobs, and I have lost some opportunities. Losing is always more pain than winning is pleasure.

There may be times when the win/lose situation is set up for us and there isn't much we can do about it. But as much as possible we should minimize those conditions and aim for win/ win situations. In terms of our material blessings, rather than setting some standard of income or net worth, like a high jumper sets his bar at a certain height, why don't we see what we can gain from our present financial situation? Setting internal goals is fine, but trying to keep up with the Joneses or even the so-called American lifestyle adds pressure and the potential for loss. We needn't bring this loss upon ourselves. There will always be some-body richer than we are, and most people in America can look around the world and see poorer people. Further, as we all know in our more rational moments, there are great lessons to be learned from struggle and economic hardship. Why call those loss? Why not call them another form of winning?

The same is true of our health and well-being. If we define perfect physical conditioning as winning, and everything short of that as losing, we will inevitably lose. The bacteria, the viruses, the accidents and physical misfortunes of the world will win. Instead, we should suck the sting of loss out of our physical handicaps. Jack Nelson, a friend of mine, was a fine athlete in high school. Just before graduation he was stricken with a disease that left his legs paralyzed. Most people would have seen this as a loss of mobility. It was, but Jack saw it as a win for wisdom. He continued to develop his fine mind and his charismatic personality. He was voted one of the preferred men on campus at college. He got his bachelor's degree and advanced degrees. He is a fine writer and teacher, a great father, a bishop, and an inspiration to all of us who know him. Not only does Jack win, but he also makes winners out of all his friends. We win just by being around him.

I believe that the cosmic win/lose battle for exaltation does not exist either, except in our minds. Fortunately for us, God is not a scorekeeper waiting to see whether we tallied enough points to win the game of life. The concept of loss does exist in the eternal economy—it is possible to lose blessings, lose membership, lose promised rewards. But loss is not the basis on which the Lord's system operates. The Lord does not participate in competition. He is cooperating with us, not competing against us. When we win he wins, and when we lose he loses. It is his work and glory to bring to pass our immortality and eternal life.

Satan would have us believe that he is a competitor in the contest, but he is not. He is at best an outside heckler. If we should lose all and end up in his dominions, it would not be a win for him. His abode is a howling anarchy of miserable souls in which there is no glory, no power, no dominion. Increasing the population of hell does not add to Satan's glory.

Ultimately, life is a win/win, not a win/lose proposition. The fewer competitions and the more cooperations we establish in our lives here, the happier we will be, and the fewer losses we will suffer. We will make more progress on our own eternal journey and better assist those about us on their way. We will see, as the Apostle Paul described, that the journey of eternal life is a different kind of race. Paul wrote that in earthly races "one receiveth the prize," but that in the eternal race all can win. So let us work on winning and forget loss as an alternative.

Chapter 21

Self-Inflicted Loss

His watery eyes flicked constantly back and forth. His red eye-lids blinked often, not so much to clear his sight as to clear his mind. At least that was the impression he gave me. He talked quite rapidly, but there were frequent pauses as he gathered his thoughts. His fingers rubbed the broom in his hand as he spoke. His face was deeply lined and his shoulders hunched. He coughed frequently. "I once owned a thriving electrical contracting busi-ness," he said. "I had a beautiful wife, a lovely family, a fine home, and the respect of my colleagues, my fellow church mem-bers, and the people in our community. I was healthy and could work long hours without getting tired. One reason I was so suc-cessful as an electrical contractor was my virtually photographic memory. I could glance at the schematic for a complicated elec-trical job, go to work, and never have to look back at it again. I could quote long passages of poetry and prose without effort. I had everything; maybe I had too much.

"I thought some of the thrills of life were passing me by, so I started to look for them in alcohol and drugs. One thing led to another until one morning I woke up literally facedown in the gutter on the waterfronts of Oakland, California. The truth slowly seeped into my brain that morning that I was a bum. I had lost everything. My business was bankrupt—my house, property, and reputation all gone. My wife had divorced me for very good reasons and taken the children with her. My health was shot, and my brain was foggy. I had nothing. I lifted up my head, laid it on the side of that gutter, and said, 'I can't get any lower than this.' "

The causes for loss in this world are too many and too varied for us to ever discover them all. Diseases that strike one person and not another, the domino effect that the failure of one business can have on others, the inevitable loss of faculties that comes with age, the coincidence that can bring two cars to a point of impact, the built-in hazards of a technological society, random bolts of lightning, and the aimless twists and turns of tornadoes are all part of the win-and-lose lottery we buy into when we are born into this world. They are often hard to endure at the time and hard to understand even in retrospect. We just get through them.

But there is one form of loss that brings with it not only grief, sadness, and bereavement but often guilt, remorse, and self-condemnation. This is the self-inflicted loss we bring on through our own sins and stupidity. I am not speaking of poor judgment, but of wrong things we do even though we know better.

This is a sensitive area studded with possibilities for misinterpretation. In terms of others' losses and misfortunes, it is usually none of our business whether they were self-caused. Bishops are set apart as common judges in Israel. It is part of their heavy responsibility to analyze and assess the causes for personal misfortunes and offer counsel and comfort to those who have suffered them. The rest of us usually do not know the facts or have the spirit of discernment to understand them. Ironically, sometimes the more we know of a situation, the less we understand. Our judgment may be clouded by our personal relationships with those who have suffered. If the afflicted person is a relative or close friend, we may feel like, and in fact may be, a part of the problem. This can impair our judgment.

Over the years I have talked to a number of parents whose children are in trouble. Often they feel that the fault is with the school or the peer group or the church or the police. Their own child is a helpless victim of circumstance. Understandably, their deep love for their child clouds their analysis of the problem and hides from them the self-inflicted aspects of the loss. Unfortunately, they sometimes spend precious energies and attention seeking retribution when they might better expend their efforts on sympathy, understanding, and assistance for their child in his loss. Sometimes we know too much and stand too close to the problem to evaluate it accurately.

Our evaluation is usually no more accurate from a distance. In this case we have the advantage of objectivity and greater perspective on the problem, but usually we don't have the facts. For example, a few years ago the media sketchily reported the tragic murder of a young woman in a convenience store. Some people hastily jumped to the conclusion that this woman was somewhat to blame for the loss of her life. Everybody knows that those places can be hangouts for hoodlums and crazies at night, they assumed. She should have been safely at home with her husband and family. Only later did the press elaborate that her two daughters and a friend were out in the car while she was renting a videotape for their entertainment. Her husband was away for the night leading his troop of Boy Scouts on an overnight outing. The gunman was crazy on drugs, anxious to kill the first human being he saw in the store. It happened to be the young mother.

We never know all the facts about other people's losses. Even if we have a detailed description of what happened outwardly, we don't know the inner battles of the mind and heart. We don't know the past histories and the environmental pressures acting on other people. Sometimes as a judge or a member of a jury, we are required to assess the actions of others. In those cases we learn all we can, pray for guidance, and hope we are accurate in our assessment. In most other instances, we need to avoid judging at all.

We sometimes understand our own situations no better than we do those of others. As a bishop I once counseled a bereaved father who was heaping guilt upon his own head for the sins of his son. He was magnifying the real loss resulting from his child's unvirtuous life by including his own imminent damnation for neglect. But I knew he was not guilty of those sins. He had done the best that a father could. I suggested he read section 68 in the Doctrine and Covenants, which specifically describes the parameters of parenthood regarding our responsibilities to our children. If we do not train up a child in light and truth, the sins are upon the heads of the parents. But I take that to mean also that if we do train up our children in light and truth, as this man had done, and they deliberately decide to go astray, the sin is not upon the heads of the parents. This man was suffering terrible loss, but it was not self-inflicted.

I have seen the young and the not-so-young flagellate themselves for losing a game or a job or a contest. "If only I had said this or done that or performed in this way, things would have been different," they say. The truth usually is that they gave it their best shot. They just came up against a team, an opponent, or a challenge that was a bit more than they could handle. There is no cause for self-recrimination in that situation. In fact, they should be complimented for biting off all they could chew and then a little bit more. The next time they may do better.

A few years ago, the aspiring Brigham Young University Cougar football program met up with Ohio State University in a post-season bowl game. Ohio State was as good as they usually are, but had dropped a couple of games in the course of the season. They were anxious to prove they were the best team in the nation. They were more than a team; they were a buzz saw, chewing up the hapless Cougars something like 47–17, as I recall. The fans mourned over this tragedy. Coach LaVell Edwards did not. He said, "We like to play good teams like this. They help us to get better, and we can get a lot better."

If we have sincerely prepared and performed to the best of our ability, we needn't add to the pain of our loss by self-recrimination. On the other hand, we sometimes shun the responsibility that is truly ours for a loss sustained. We want to blame others, our environment, our background, our history. We are like the little boy who handed his less-than-sterling report card to his father and said, "What's the matter with me, Dad? Is it heredity or environment?" Some people even reach out into the universe and blame their shortcomings on the astrological alignment of stars and planets. To them, Shakespeare speaks in the words of Cassius to Brutus in the play *Julius Caesar*. In the midst of some grumbling and grousing that Caesar was born lucky and that was why he was emperor and they were not, Cassius said truthfully, "The fault, dear Brutus, is not in our stars, but in ourselves, that we are underlings."

The tragedy of not seeing our self-inflicted losses is that we lose doubly. We sustain the original loss, and we also lose the opportunity to learn from it. Judgment of self and others is difficult, and the Lord counseled extreme caution: "For with what judgment ye judge, ye shall be judged." (Matthew 7:2.) But there are times when we know from outward evidence and our own inner conviction that, in fact, our loss was self-inflicted. We have acted unwisely or sinfully and brought misfortune upon ourselves. Why we do these things is a matter of only oblique relevance to this short discussion. Psychologists speculate that we sometimes have a death wish; we choose to fail. We may get a thrill from seeing how close to the edge of the cliff we can stand; when we do this, sometimes the cliff crumbles beneath us or the wind blows us over. We may feel that we are smart enough to beat the odds, and that what causes loss in others will not cause it in us. Often selfishness, pride, or temptations of the flesh enter into our actions. Whatever the cause, we look up one day and find we have lost our fortune, our self-image, or the love and respect of friends and spouse. Or we may have lost our health, our mental capacities, or our opportunities to succeed.

My alcoholic friend in Oakland, California, was almost as complete a loss as I can conceive of in this world, but even this man's abject condition was not a total wipeout. Deep within him was a tiny, glowing ember, a weak and distant trace of memory, a dim and fuzzy picture of what he once had been. He could vaguely feel the man he had been, not only in this life, I believe, but in his previous existence when he stood as a spirit child of God. Somewhere deep inside he knew he was more than a dissipated derelict, a wasted animal. That memory was all he had left, but it was enough to give him the strength to lift his knees up onto the sidewalk, struggle groggily to his feet, and begin to shuffle slowly along the road back.

Back? No, he was not taking the road back. This is one of our most common mistakes in self-inflicted loss: we try to turn and take the road back. As an old eastern proverb has it, "You can never step in the same river twice." In this life the clock only turns one way. We blind ourselves to our future destination when we move forward with our eyes looking over our shoulders. My wasted friend, for all his mistakes and misjudgments, realized this. As far as I know, he never regained his family and his prosperity. His fine mind was a fraction of its former self. He lived alone and worked at a menial but honest job. He was humble and faithful in his church duties and kind to everyone he met. He said to me, "I'm not where I was when I was up, but I'm a long way from where I was when I was down."

No matter how heavy is our personal responsibility for our loss or the burden we bear from it, we can always move forward and upward. There is a program for making this progress. It is called repentance. There are also any number of imitations that promise relief, but cannot deliver it. Only repentance can put us back on the path of progress. This purging process can sometimes be painful, but it is not nearly as painful and debilitating as the sins that made it necessary. And the pain is the kind that accompanies healing.

Although repentance is hard, it is not complicated. It consists simply of recognizing our errors, turning from them, and making restitution to the best of our ability for whatever damage we have done. True repentance requires that we beg the forgiveness of any whom we have offended. Whether they choose to forgive us is up to them, but our repentance is not contingent on how they respond. We are not dependent on anyone else to exercise true repentance. We have the power within ourselves to begin the repentance process and to call upon God's Spirit to complete it. For it is in our Father's hands that the healing process ultimately rests. He it is whom we first grieved when we sinned, and it is he to whom we return with our broken heart and contrite spirit so he can forgive us and make us whole again. He has promised us that he will do so: "As often as my people repent will I forgive their trespasses against me." (Mosiah 26:30.)

We may sometimes feel we have sunk so low that we have lost everything, including the Lord's love and the opportunity to repent. This is a doctrine of the champion of discouragement, even Satan himself. He would have us believe that we are not worth saving, but that is not true. The Lord has specifically designated only two sins for which there is no forgiveness: denial of the Holy Ghost and the shedding of innocent blood. Even these are beyond repentance not because of God, but because of the nature of the sins. God is never so offended by his children that he slams the door and ignores their sincere pleadings to enter. But when we slam the door to him and refuse to open it, he cannot be with us. Those who commit the unpardonable sins have tasted to the fullest the love and the power of God. They have found it bitter and spat it out. God has no further ways to reach them. He will force no man. So if we choose to be unforgiven, we shall be. To any repentant sinner who knocks — though it be the gentlest of taps with feeble, bloody, sin-stained knuckles — the Lord will hear and open.

Self-inflicted loss is the bitterest loss of all, but even this can be overcome.

Chapter 22

Gaining through Loss

Stephen Blake was a handsome, popular, and talented young man. He had been a high school student-body officer and a missionary. Few young men have a brighter future before them. But standing on a street corner one day, he glanced up to see a crane hit the wires of a 7200–volt power line. The two men operating the crane below were immediately frozen to the machinery and in danger of being electrocuted.

No one would have criticized Stephen Blake for standing helplessly by. People would have commended him had he run away and gone for help. But he instinctively knew there was not time for that, so he ran to the crisis. He pulled the two men free and saved their lives, but in the process he was trapped in the grip of the electricity. By the time the power line was shut down, he was in a coma from which he never recovered. He voluntarily lost what many people would consider to be his most valuable possession, his earthly life. From the narrow perspective of this world, he lost his life in exchange for a few words of eulogy at a funeral and the gratitude of the men he saved.

Weighed on the balance scales of eternity, the transaction looks different. Jesus said, "Greater love hath no man than this, that a man lay down his life for his friends." (John 15:13.) Stephen Blake exhibited even greater love than that by which a man lays down his life for his friend. He laid down his life for strangers — two men he didn't know and to whom he had no obligation, except that they were his brothers in the human family. To be assayed in the Lord's value system and found to be pure celestial material, as he was—is that not worth even the loss of his remaining years in this earthly life?

Semantics sometimes throws monkey wrenches into our thinking mechanisms. We mistake the name for the thing—the symbol for the referent. Such may be the case when we consider loss. *Loss* means by definition to have something taken from us—to have less than we had before. But even if this definition is technically correct, is it misleading and myopic? Frequently, that depends on the depth and breadth of our understanding. We don't often console a baby when it loses the opportunity to be carried because it learns to walk. Although being carried is more comfortable, walking is a stage in growth that most of us would not want to do without. We sometimes mourn the loss of our youth, but few people—Peter Pan notwithstanding—would really want to be children forever. The adventures, satisfactions, and wisdom of maturity are worth the price we pay in lost childhood.

According to the scriptures, the human race itself and this world in its present state were launched by way of a loss. Adam and Eve lost their innocence, their ignorance, and their home in the weedless Garden of Eden when they partook of the forbidden fruit. At first it may have seemed to them that they got little in return. They were driven from their beautiful garden into a lonely and desolate world. In place of fruits and flowers, they saw thorns and thistles. Their honeymoon in Eden was over; ahead of them lay the sweat of the brow for Adam and travail in childbirth for Eve. They may have felt their loss was bitter indeed, but without this loss they would have remained forever in their state of childish innocence and inexperience.

Their condition was a type and shadow of our own. Like the snake bound up in his old skin, we get bound to our present possessions and satisfied with our present situation. Sometimes we have to shed this old skin to allow us room to grow. From this perspective loss, gain, and retention become harder to define.

At one time Brigham Young sent three eighteen-year-old men

into the Wyoming wilderness to help a starving handcart company reach the valley of the Great Salt Lake. The three boys found the company huddled on the far shore of an icy, swollen river. Without hesitation, they crossed the stream and brought back their weary brothers and sisters one at a time in their arms. The handcart company was saved, but the boys paid a great price. The strain was so terrible, and the exposure so great, that in later years all the boys died from the effects of it. When President Brigham Young heard of this heroic act, he wept like a child, and he later declared publicly, "That act alone will ensure C. Allen Huntington, George W. Grant, and David P. Kimball an everlasting salvation in the Celestial Kingdom of God, worlds without end."

To have achieved the selflessness and character of these young men, as did Stephen Blake, and thus assured ourselves of an inheritance in the kingdom of God with our loved ones—this is the true measure of loss and gain in our lives. Anything that contributes to that ultimate end is a gain, even if it involves a temporary loss. Anything that detracts from our winning that crown is a loss, even though it may produce a temporary financial, social, or power gain in this world.

We may not recover from a financial crash in this life; we may not get back lost health; power and position may slip through our fingers; friends may prove false; and all manner of so-called losses may befall us, beyond our control. But the ultimate measure of loss and gain is within our control. If we falter, err, or sin and lose a portion of our inheritance, the Lord has promised us that we can repent and have it restored to us. We can even turn it to our gain if we learn from the experience to become more righteous and more understanding of those about us who need our help. It is only as we deliberately choose not to repent that such a loss becomes permanent to us. That is indeed a sad thing.

Let us not be too quick to judge an apparent misfortune as a loss. Let us turn it to a gain whenever we can. When we indeed do suffer a loss from our own doing, let us repent quickly so that in the final judgment all that we have done will have been toward progress and perfection.

Chapter 23

Loss Can Give Us Perspective

"I would that ye should remember, and always retain in remembrance, the greatness of God, and your own nothingness, and his goodness and long-suffering towards you, unworthy creatures, and humble yourselves even in the depths of humility." (Mosiah 4:11.) These scriptural words of warning and exhortation remind us to beware of pride. Most of us would nod our heads in agreement with such a warning. In principle, if not always in practice, we can recognize the dangers of pride and vanity—particularly in the lives of others. From King Saul in the Bible to King Lear in Shakespeare, history and literature are full of examples of individuals and nations who had good things going for them until pride overcame them and became their downfall.

The ancient Greeks saw pride as part of a four-step process. They called it *hubris*, and they connected it conceptually with the act of eating. The first step in this process is to feel hunger; the second is to take the steps to satisfy that hunger; the third is to stuff the old stomach. This is where *hubris* comes in, and here is the danger point. If a person does not have control over his appetite, he will continue to stuff beyond his physical needs, and even beyond his capacity to hold. This can bring on the fourth stage. It can be as simple and short-lived as regurgitating what we have just eaten. Or, if the effects accumulate sufficiently, it can be as permanent as a fatal heart attack brought on by overweight.

As with any analogy, this comparison of eating and living breaks down if we push it too far. But it does point out some truths we might not see in another context. In this case we see more clearly the critical point in our aspirations. The ancients had no quarrel with people recognizing their hungers, their need for better things. They admired, as we often do, people trying to improve their lot through their physical, social, psychological, or spiritual desires. But they recognized, as we do, that once the table is spread before us, we do not automatically use wisdom about when to stop or what to eat. We sometimes gorge ourselves to destruction.

King Saul of ancient Israel had few needs for glory and popularity as a young man. He was a tall and handsome man, standing a full head above his fellows – kingly in his bearing. But he came from a humble home in one of the smallest tribes of Israel, the tribe of Benjamin. He was a farm boy, and so shy about being called a king that when they went to anoint him, he had, as the Bible said, "hid himself among the stuff." The prophet Samuel had to go dig him out and drag him up before the people. But Saul soon developed an appetite for kingly glory. When the people began to divert their applause and acclaim from King Saul to the young warrior David, it tore Saul up. He became a pitiful paranoid. He tried to kill David, and eventually took his own life. Saul was a classic example of the dangers of pride.

Shakespeare, with his unparalleled insight into human foibles, gave us another clear case in the aging King Lear. Lear is a fairly acceptable king, as kings go, but he has an insatiable hunger for affection and adoration, particularly from his daughters. Two of them are willing to pander to his neurotic needs in order to help satisfy their own selfish desires. The third daughter is too honest to lie to her father. She loves him and pays him the compliment of an honest relationship. But Lear demands more than this, disdains his true daughter's love, and turns to those he hopes will heap the table for his emotional gluttony.

Lear's lack of control is his undoing, as would be the case with all of us. Soon he loses the power to demand love and attention. When his supply of fawning adoration is cut off, he starves emotionally and goes insane. Only his true daughter still cares for him, but he is too crazy to notice very much. Lear's tragedy is twofold. First, he suffers from uncontrolled desires. Second, and perhaps even more tragic, he has the power and authority to command that those desires be fulfilled.

In real history King Henry VIII of England suffered the same deprivation of discipline when he was growing up. His doting father commanded that the young prince be given everything he wanted. Nothing was to be denied him, so that he might know from the first that he was a king. As a result, Henry enjoyed a childhood that might be envied by any kid who ever pressed his nose against the window of a store and looked at things he couldn't afford. But King Henry paid for his undisciplined childhood with a dissipated adulthood that would be envied by no king or commoner in his right mind. He also destroyed the lives of those about him, including several wives, and destroyed his own mind and body with syphilis.

Naturally, Henry attracted about him those of like disposition. Cardinal Thomas Wolsey, Henry's right-hand henchman in religious matters, suffered a sobering comeuppance and a crashing downfall from his own overarching ambition. Shakespeare has Wolsey sum up his rise and fall in these profound words:

> . . . *I have ventur'd,*
> *Like little wanton boys on bladders,*
> *This many summers in a sea of glory;*
> *But far beyond my depth: my high-blown pride*
> *At length broke under me; and now has left me,*
> *Weary and old with service, to the mercy*
> *Of a rude stream, that must for ever hide me. . . .*
>
> *Had I but serv'd my God with half the zeal*
> *I serv'd my king, he would not in mine age*
> *Have left me naked to mine enemies.*

These unfortunate victims of their own *hubris* are not different animals from you and me, but they had the misfortune to possess the means to gorge themselves on the poison of pride. It destroyed them.

To help us guard against this tragedy in our own lives, the Lord has blessed us with times of loss. If our material comforts were guaranteed to us for life, we might be even more prone to hoard them and to ignore the riches of eternity the Lord has counseled us to seek. If the applause for our activities never stopped, but continued to build, round upon round, throughout our lives, would not our pride fatten to ugly proportions on this food while our humility and empathy for others dwindled and starved? If we never lost our youth, would we not continue to glut ourselves on the bravado and narcissism that are so characteristic of those early years? If we never lost a loved one, would we ever turn our eyes from the temporary relationships of this world and fix them on the eternal relationships of the next?

In our more sober moments of contemplation, we should give thanks for the losses in our lives because they help to set limits on our *hubris* — our insatiable appetite for pride and the temptations of this world. These are limits that need to be set, but we are usually loath to set them ourselves. And so the losses of our lives are often temporary setbacks to save us from permanent, self-inflicted destruction.

Chapter 24

Loss, or Change?

· ·

Back in 1949, Brent Scowcroft's P-51 fighter plane lost power and crashed, ending his flying career and almost ending his life. The Ogden, Utah, native spent the next two years in hospital beds. He lost his chances to soar among the clouds and had to resign himself to a military desk job. It would have been easy to ground his aspirations along with his body. But he refused. Instead, he made his career soar until he became national security adviser of the United States. He reinterpreted his loss and turned it into a change of direction.

Life is structured such that we almost never gain something without losing something else. We cannot gain the wisdom of maturity without suffering the loss of youth. If we gain new friends, we usually lose some of the intimacy and intensity we had with our old ones. There isn't enough time for both. Gaining popularity and fame means a loss of anonymity and the privacy that accompanies it. I have sat through concerts with trained musicians. I think I often enjoyed the music more than they did because they had lost that bright-eyed, naive joy of the novice. Subconsciously, they were analyzing and evaluating when they might have been just blissfully enjoying if they had not lost their aesthetic innocence. But in the trade they had gained a deeper understanding for parts of the music that I missed.

Jesus used an analogy of a kernel of wheat to explain this principle. Except the wheat be lost and placed in the ground, it can never bring forth abundant sheaves. The same is true with all of us. We cannot gain eternal life without losing our temporal lives. The Lord counseled us to deliberately lose our lives. He said, "He that findeth his life shall lose it: and he that loseth his life for my sake shall find it." (Matthew 10:39.)

The loss of something we treasure, whether it is material, social, or physical, is usually a painful experience. But the sting can be softened, and sometimes removed altogether, when we think of the experience not as loss but as change. Whether the change is for better or for worse depends upon us.

Probably no caterpillar in the world would voluntarily give up his mobility in crawling and seal himself up in a cocoon. He doesn't know that beautiful wings and soaring flight await him on the other side of his loss. Life for us is not so predictable. It is not always obvious what we shall be after the metamorphosis of loss has changed us. We ourselves have much to say about what those changes will bring.

Mark Twain had been a successful writer. He was acclaimed in his native America and in Europe. He had a lovely wife and three loving daughters. Within thirteen years, his wife and two of his daughters died. He said, "How poor I am who was once so rich!" His experience would appear to be the butterfly transition in reverse. He saw himself transformed from a flying, free spirit to a crawling, downcast grub. Such losses as his could easily bring on such an outlook. But how much comfort he could have obtained had he been able to see change instead of only loss—if he had seen his wife changed from mortality to immortality, his daughters saved much of the pain and suffering of this world and taken to a better one. He could have seen his own changed state as a chance to explore more deeply the problems and struggles of his fellow beings and portray them with his literary genius. Thus he might have changed through his loss from a witty, insightful observer of human foibles to a sensitive humanitarian. He might have exchanged his caustic cynicism for a sustaining faith in the Lord. Such changes do not come automatically from a loss, but they can be wrested from the ashes of tragedy.

One of the finest illustrations of turning loss into change for the better is the story of *Silas Marner* by George Eliot. Marner is a greedy skinflint, intent only on gathering possessions for himself. He hoards his time, emotions, and possessions, and especially his precious gold. But one night a thief steals his treasure. Marner is crushed, disconsolate. He has lost his gold. He has no friends, helpers, or sympathizers because he has developed none. All his interest was in his gold, and now it is gone.

Some time later he awakes to a knock on his door, peers suspiciously out, and sees on his doorstep something gold wrapped in blankets and placed in a bundle in a basket. "My gold is returned," he cries in joy. As it turns out, it is better gold than the gold he lost. It is the golden tresses of a baby girl, who has been placed on his doorstep to be cared for. The scene is rich with symbolism. One of the less obvious but significant aspects is Marner's mistaking golden hair for gold. Most people would not be confused by the two even for a moment, but Marner's eye is so single to material things that he has developed not a Midas touch, but a Midas look. He searches for gold in everything. Some people's viewpoint gets that narrow and skewed. Human relationships, experiences, earth beauties, and resources are looked at as an assayer analyzes ore for the monetary value in it.

The sight of the baby triggers the beginnings of a change in Silas Marner. He takes her in and cares for her. He gives and sacrifices for her, as any parent must, and eventually rears her into a beautiful and loving young woman. In the process his heart also opens up to friends, neighbors, and others in need. Silas Marner, the selfish skinflint, turns into Silas Marner, the loving father and devoted friend to all mankind. It is obvious that he has not lost his treasure but unwillingly invested it and reaped richer returns than he could have ever dreamed.

Much of the loss in our own lives is similar to Silas Marner's. If we respond to it in the right way, we will later look back and see it not as loss but as a change and a blessing. What, then, is the right way, the right response? First of all, the right way to respond to loss, I believe, is to face it squarely. It is not by accident that the author used the symbolism of gold to illustrate both Silas Marner's loss and the trigger for his beginnings of change. I believe if Marner had mourned the loss of his gold but then found comfort in something else—nature or books or solitary contemplation, for instance—the story would have lost much of its impact. The dark world and the enlightened world of Silas Marner had to touch at exactly the same geographical point if he were to make the transition from one into the other. The symbolism is somewhat like Michelangelo's famous painting of God and Adam on the ceiling of the Sistine Chapel. God, from his glorified and exalted position, reaches down. Adam, from below, reaches up. Their fingers touch. Through that contact, like an electrical connection, you can almost see the power of God flowing into his son Adam.

And thus it is with us. The sharp, painful point of our loss is exactly the appendage with which we must probe to touch the new world of change. It is not a natural response. Our tendency is to pad over the point of pain, to hope that it scabs and eventually heals. But it will not. It will only fester and continue to grieve us. Some people who have lost a loved one continue to live as though the passing never happened. This hampers their personal relationships and their continued emotional, spiritual, and sometimes even intellectual growth. Some who have lost a limb subconsciously try to hide the fact. They find frustration in trying to be exactly the way they were and having their mental construct not match their physical condition.

One of the most courageous and wise handicapped people I ever knew was a little boy in our children's elementary school. He had been born with a serious cleft palate. His mouth was misshapen, and his speech was nasal and slurred. But that did not hold him back. Every time I would meet him and talk with him, he would thrust his lip forward and let me and the world know that he knew his point of pain and was making no secret of it. If you wanted his friendship, you had to take him mouth first. Before long, I found out it was a privilege to do so. He is now a dynamic and successful man, a great contributor to his family, his church, his business, and the community.

Some people who lose material blessings can't bring themselves to face that loss and continue to live as though nothing had happened. Instead of facing their loss and making it the focal point of change for the better, they squander their remaining resources to keep up appearances to others and to themselves.

The first step in turning loss into change is to stare the loss straight in the eyes. Make it blink and back away. The first thing you will find as you do so is that the loss is not as total as you had supposed. The universe is still functioning, and you are still breathing. The heat of your gaze will peel away the mists and the mysteries, the fears and the uncertainties of your loss, and expose it for what it is. It is a sadness, a difficulty, a challenge, but it is not a paralyzing power that can overwhelm you. You and the Lord are capable of overcoming and subduing any loss.

The second step is to use this close analysis of your loss to see what, in fact, is the focal point of the pain and how that point can be used as a prod to change. We almost lost one of our sons to drugs and riotous living. My first response was to try to deal with the situation quietly – to ignore it, not only with the neighbors and people in church but in my dealings with my son. I wanted to talk about other things and hope that this demon of drugs hovering over our relationship would just go away. It didn't. We had to face it squarely, analyze what we had lost, which was considerable, and then see how we could turn that loss to change.

Looking at his loss carefully, my son decided he must change, take more control of his own life, and not let bad friends and the momentary euphoria of drugs direct his destiny. For my part, I found that the pain brought change in my theories and practices as a father. I became less exacting, more concerned with the spirit than the letter of the law, more concerned with my son's needs and desires, and less concerned with what other people might think about us.

I am constrained to believe that with the Lord as our guide and comfort, and with the proper attitude, there is no loss in this life, only change. If we will it to be so, the change will be for the better.

Epilogue

Your Loss and
Your Eternal Journey

. . . .

You have traveled far on your eternal journey, just in the reading of these few pages. You are not the same person you were when you opened the book. Even at this moment, your progress continues.

Nothing stands still in life, and nothing repeats. Our sun, which seems so constant with its repetitious rising, is in fact hurtling through space at a thousand miles a minute and taking us along. Our galaxy, in turn, is streaking across the universe fulfilling the measure of its creation.

The cycling seasons are not circles at all, but spirals taking us up or down with each year's passing. Our direction up or down the spiral depends upon the set of our guidance systems. Whatever adjustments we make in our lives are in-flight corrections. There is no way to stand still while we decide which direction we should go.

Your loss will not stop your journey, but it will probably affect your direction. It may turn your gaze upward toward the eternal beacons that beckon us back to the presence of God and our own godliness. Or your loss may tempt you to look forever back to the better times, or down into the dust of discouragement. Only you can decide the set of your face, the angle of your eyes, the direction and the destination of your journey.

I hope the essays and instructions in this book will comfort and encourage you along your upward climb through life. You carry within you the power to grow, and the inexhaustible powers of heaven are available to you. These are strength sufficient to carry you along your way one step, one day, one year at a time. Godspeed you.

Index